"In my role as a wor[...] professional, I am increas[...] leave their jobs as they strive for more wo[...] balance. It is an employee's market, as doors continue to open with new opportunities that allow more flexibility. During the time of the "Great Resignation," employers must be purposeful and aggressive about both recruiting and retaining talent. This book provides practical strategies to create a positive workplace culture and imparts simple tools to reduce turnover and establish a team that feels valued."

—**Jessica Belitz**, Director of Workforce Development, Blount Partnership

"From day one of founding my company, I knew the importance of creating a culture that drives success, but I didn't know the HOW. Brenda and Amanda share all the secrets to create a culture that drives both business success and success of your individual employees. Relationships and connections are what make businesses thrive; that's why the practical and effective strategies shared in this book are pivotal in your business success. Brenda and Amanda have left no stone unturned in *The Retention Process*; it's your key to team success. Invest in your team (starting with this book), and they will invest in your clients and company. When you get the process right, you won't have to worry about your bottom line. It will take care of itself."

—**Denae Hively**, Founder of The Hively Co

"Compliance is more than following the rules for the sake of rules. It speaks volumes to your team and clients about their worth. In *The Retention Process*, Amanda and Brenda share the importance compliance plays in retaining valuable and highly engaged employees. With integrated tools and strategies, this book is a must-read for all companies looking to grow their business through the retention of productive employees."

—**Helen Izek**, Business Compliance Manager; editor; and author of *The Red Road Home*

"Brenda has always been able to discuss hard stuff with a refreshing and inspiring outlook. I appreciate how she and Amanda bring feelings into the unemotional world of business. People matter. This process to find, manage, and retain a team is an invaluable resource that we as business owners sometimes forget in our day-to-day busyness. This is a poignant and helpful reminder to look up every now and then to pour into your people! People need to be heard, valued, respected, feel intelligent, useful, and appreciated and get paid for it. Having been in sales and marketing in the same area for almost twenty years, I see these simple truths get thrown away in the pursuit of success. So, thank you, Brenda and Amanda, for bringing the essentials back to the forefront of business . . . where it belongs!"

—**Dawn Rhodes**, Realtor, Insurance Broker Rhodes lLife & Health, Chandler Chamber Board Member, Leadership Tyler Class 20

THE RETENTION PROCESS

CREATE A CULTURE OF
WORTH IN THE WORKPLACE

Other Books by the Authors

The Team Solution Series

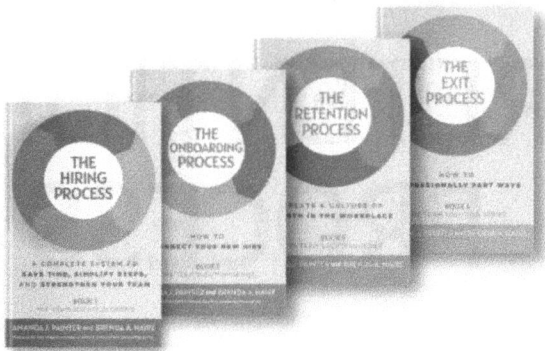

The Author Solution Series

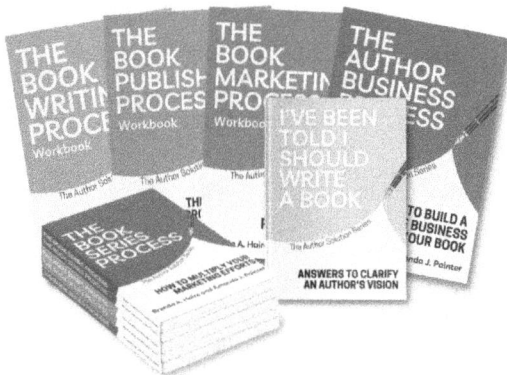

Also by Brenda A. Haire

TheJoyOfPursuit.com

THE RETENTION PROCESS

CREATE A CULTURE OF
WORTH IN THE WORKPLACE

AMANDA J. PAINTER

and

BRENDA A. HAIRE

BOOK 3
THE TEAM SOLUTION SERIES

Joy*of* **PURSUIT**
PUBLISHING

Throughout the book, you'll be introduced to new tools. We provide assessments, templates, worksheets, and more.

Download your free bundle at theJoyOfPursuit.com/Retention

@JoyofPursuit

Dedication

We dedicate this book to those pouring their lives into a Vision bigger than themselves. We see you. We value you. May the culture you're in rise to meet you and take you further than you ever dreamed.

Contents

Foreword

Our culture is constantly changing, and if we're not intentional about how we show up in the world, it can change us too. Workplace culture is no different. I've been an entrepreneur long enough to know that I don't ever want to work for someone else again, and that I want to create a positive environment for anyone working with me.

I've been a full-time blogger since 2011. This didn't happen by letting the world around me dictate how I showed up. So, what did I do differently? Be intentional! I intentionally read books that educated me and surrounded myself with people that opened my eyes to possibilities and allowed me to shine in my grace-given gifts.

In this book, authors Brenda and Amanda are asking you to be intentional. Create a workplace of worth where your team can shine. Open their eyes to what is possible if they come alongside you as a leader and devote the majority of their waking hours to your vision. *The Retention Process* isn't a book of fluff or chalked full of stories to inspire you to do better. It is a practical guide packed with usable tools that will help you create a culture your team thrives in.

You'll discover clarity around what you do and how to share your Mission with your team in a way that honors them and what they bring to the table. This is Book 3 in *The Team Solution Series: HR Coaching to Grow Teams and Profit*, and each book focuses on the importance of communication and validation. This book breaks down communication to the point of telling you where and how to properly communicate and what to stop doing that is irritating your team. It's time, as leaders, we step up and actually care about how our team feels about working with us. Employee retention is much more than saving the company money, and while that is important for profitability, you need to understand the bigger picture.

You need to implement this book's process, yesterday. Your team deserves it. You deserve it! You've invested a lot to get where you are, don't squander it now. I'd suggest you grab a copy for everyone on your team so they all understand you value them and want to create a place they are excited about growing with for years to come.

Amanda and Brenda guide you through the process beautifully. Trust the process.

Jonathan Milligan,
Online Business Owner, Author, Marketing Coach at Market Your Message

A Note to You—the Reader

To win in the marketplace
you must first win in the workplace.

—Doug Conant

Welcome to the third book in *The Team Solution Series.* Since this book is about culture, we will share more personal stories and examples from our experiences in the workplace. We want you to not only learn the process for retention but also understand the emotion behind it.

Retention is a fragile process. When dealing with your team, it's important to remember that they are *emotional* beings; everyone experiences emotions differently. This is where your own emotional intelligence will be tested and shaped. While we won't get mushy enough to make you cry, we may step on some toes.

You'll hear about our passion for change and our hearts for equipping your team to better serve your clients—because both matter. People matter. *Kindness* matters. If you get this process right, you won't have to worry about your bottom line. It will take care of itself.

>>>>>

Amanda started her entrepreneurial journey early. As a child, she sold lemonade from a wooden stand one of the neighborhood dads made. Her first paying job at age sixteen was at a new pizza restaurant, but she quickly realized that welcoming customers into a fast-food restaurant wasn't her cup of tea. After four short, greasy months, she joined the staff at a big-box office supply store, where she worked throughout high school and college. Creating an engaged and long-term employee out of a teenager is no easy task, but someone there clearly understood employee retention.

Brenda's older sister, Jenifer, taught her more about perseverance in business than anyone she knows. Together, they ventured into the business world long before their first jobs. They didn't "play school" as some girls did. Following the adult examples in their lives, they played office or pretended to run a restaurant in their dad's backyard greenhouse. Her first paying job was sweeping up hair at a salon owned by a family member. Later, she became the receptionist, answering the phone and scheduling appointments. She was only twelve or thirteen at the time.

Jenifer says her first job was being a big sister, to which Brenda responds with a laugh. "Jenifer had her work cut out for her as *my* big sister. For her to consider her first job to be taking care of me ... I mean, cue the tears. I never thought of our relationship that way. I must have let her down so many times, but that explains why she has always been my biggest cheerleader."

Cheerleaders in the workplace remind us of multilevel marketing (MLM). You probably just cringed. It's okay; you're not alone. But you're about to learn a huge lesson to take into your workplace. Not all MLM companies (or social selling companies) are created equal, and not all uplines (the people who recruit you and make a commission from you) grasp this concept. But Brenda recalls an excellent example of leadership: a lovely lady named Shay Akin. Shay was Brenda's director in her first MLM.

Brenda explains, "She trained me, strategized with me, inspired me, included me, and most importantly, *believed* in me. She believed in me long before I believed in myself, and she was right there when I received my free car! She taught by example how to lead others well."

So, what does that have to do with your business? Well, are you strategizing with your employees, inspiring them, including them, believing in them? Most people will say that your upline in an MLM only does that because they are making a commission from you. But didn't you hire your employee to make *you* money? Sure, you did. Become your team's biggest cheerleader. It will pay off—in employee *and* income retention.

〉〉〉〉〉

Our passion for the working class and the people who employ them led us to build our company, Joy of Pursuit, to create joyful workplaces around the world. We don't believe work should only be fun for children "playing office." We recognize the joy children find in work, in exploring options, and in creating without fear. Before work was a chore, before someone belittled your ideas or barked orders with little respect, there was joy in trying new things and using your unique grace-given gifts for the sake of serving others.

In this book, we will give you the tools you need to create a culture of worth in the workplace—one that encourages joy, creativity, and exploration. With a clear Mission, consistently innovative systems, and a sincere servant's heart for your clients *and* employees, your company will make a difference while growing your bottom line.

We've all vented about bad bosses, jobs we've hated, lazy co-workers, unproductive employees, and rude clients. You name it, you've probably complained about it to a confidant. Now it's time to learn a new way to build a company, to the best of your ability, free from those headaches.

We believe in the value people bring to the workplace and recognize how their value impacts your business and community. We will guide you through ideas, principles, strategies, tools, and resources to enlighten you and your team on positioning, profitability, and preservation. You'll learn to protect your investment while promoting your team and pleasing your clients in a way that doesn't compromise your Core Values or company culture.

The key to retaining a great team, and ultimately multiplying your investment, is in

- understanding your company's Mission and communicating it with actions.
- professionally leading the right people at every level in your company.
- implementing legitimate policies and practices that support your team and Vision.
- aligning your organization, accountability, and responsibility.

The results will be

- simplified operations to maximize efficiency and communication.
- invested, committed employees in a culture of worth.
- retention of valued employees, resources, and revenue.

From *The Hiring Process* to *The Onboarding Process*, we gave you strategic tools to support employee retention and avoid turnover. With *The Retention Process,* we will discuss why employees stay or leave and how you can be intentional in creating a company culture people want to work in and with.

We provide a Workplace Culture Assessment in *The Retention Process* Toolbox. If you haven't already taken it, we encourage you to do so now. This will be a tool to share with your team when you've finished reading this book and have committed to making the changes this process outlines. If you've already committed and you're reading this book with your team, start by having everyone take the assessment so you will have a grasp on your current culture and what changes you will need to implement. Understanding if your company Mission—your most important assignment— is relevant in today's marketplace or if your team clearly understands your Mission will help you identify gaps and areas that need your attention.

Chapter One

Map to Culture

Great vision without great people is irrelevant.

—Jim Collins

Retention and culture go hand in hand. Understanding your workplace culture and how it affects your employees is the first step to retention.

People work to create better lives for themselves and their families, and they want to do so in a place that makes them feel valued and appreciated. No one enjoys a toxic environment. As employees often spend more of their waking hours each week at work than at home, they are feeling the effects of work on their health, including their mental health. Even if the employee is remote, if the culture starts to damage their mental health, they will make a shift. If the culture doesn't fit their lifestyle or goals, they will move on.

But when there is a culture of worth, team members know they are:

- Heard
- Validated
- Respected
- Knowledgeable
- Useful
- Appreciated
- Fairly compensated

The result will be:

- Team engagement
- Better communication
- Higher productivity

- Less absenteeism
- Reduced turnover
- High customer satisfaction
- Greater bottom line

Who Is Responsible for Company Culture?

Culture is a result of your values and actions. A healthy culture starts at the top and becomes an infinite cycle of respect, vulnerability, communication, and validation. Think of your company culture as a track in the shape of an infinity symbol, endlessly and smoothly continuing in a figure eight. The owner, possibly you, created the culture, but it should not end with you. The whole company should stay on track and keep it running. Any time someone on your team miscommunicates, they derail the culture. But each time they communicate well, the cycle continues in a smooth, infinite pattern.

While your company grows, your culture should consistently convey value. We'll show you how to establish that culture and keep it.

How Is Workplace Culture Created?

The terms *Mission, Vision, Purpose,* and *Core Values* often get blurred in business. In Brenda's first book, *Save the Butter Tubs!: Discover Your Worth in a Disposable World*, she shares that

Values + Action = Character
and
Values + Action = Culture

What we value and how we act on those values create our character, and many characters working together collectively create the culture in which we work and live. In business, our Company Core Components™—Mission, Purpose, Core Values, Brand Uniques, and Vision—describe what we do, why we do it, and the character we possess when we take the necessary actions to create a desired future.

Many business leaders view Company Core Components as unnecessary or fluff that looks nice on the company website. But when correctly identified, communicated well, implemented properly, and protected, Company Core Components will be the most important part of your business.

Company Core Components (CCC):

Mission is your important assignment.

Purpose is the reason for your Mission.

Core Values (CV) are the beliefs that guide your Mission.

Brand Uniques (BU) are one to three unique actions by which you achieve your Mission.

Vision is the future you're creating through your Mission.

On the next page, we provide the Company Core Components Worksheet. A printable version is available in the Toolbox. If you're writing these for the first time, collaborate with your team and get everyone on the same page from the start. If you have been in business for any length of time, you may have these documented in a business plan, your Team Handbook, or even displayed on a wall in the foyer. Now is the time to capture them all in one place and make sure they support each other.

You started your business for a reason. It started with a Vision. It's time to ask yourself some questions. Are your CCCs still relevant to the marketplace and the work you are doing? Take a moment to complete the worksheet, and as you read about the five components, add clarity where needed.

Company Core Components Worksheet

Mission + Purpose + Culture = Vision
Your What + Your Why + Your How = Results

Mission   What is our company's important assignment?
             What are we known for?
_____
_____
_____
_____

Purpose   Why does our company exist?
             Narrow the focus to one reason we do what we do.
_____
_____
_____

Core Values   What deep beliefs do we have as a company that drives what
                  we do on a daily basis? List 3–10.
_____
_____
_____
_____
_____

Brand Uniques   How do we uniquely do what we do? List up to three unique
                    actions. What sets us apart from our competition?
_____
_____
_____

Vision   Describe the future our company is striving to create through its
             work.
_____
_____
_____

Mission—Your Important Assignment

A mission statement is your business's Job Description. It's your important assignment. Nowhere in that Job Description does it say to people-please, micromanage, or change direction on a whim. Those are clearly not important assignments but the very things that will derail your company culture and distract from your Mission.

You know what your company stands for. It is not about you but about clearly solving your client's problem. What problem does your company solve for your client? Not *how* or *why*—that comes later—just the "what." *What* are you actually called to do for the people your business serves? That's your Mission.

Purpose—Your Reason

Unless you are clear on your Purpose, you'll try to be all things to all people, or you'll be distracted by shiny objects you think will bring immediate results and joy. Sadly, most shiny objects disappoint, and we've seen firsthand when they've destroyed teams, families, and entire businesses. So, how can we stay focused?

Remember your Purpose. *Why* are you doing any of this to begin with? Running a business is time-consuming, costly, stressful, and complicated. Committing to the core reason for existing as a company will not only keep you focused, but will also make room for joy.

You've stated your important assignment— your Mission; so now, ask yourself "Why?" Why is that Mission important? Why does it matter to your future client? Once you have your reason, be certain everyone in your company knows it and understands it. Will your company provide a better way for your clients? Will it save lives? Will it save people money or time? Know your "why."

Core Values—Your Beliefs

Your Core Values are the pillars of your company culture—the deeply ingrained principles that guide all actions, from marketing to hiring.

When identifying Core Values, it is vital to not confuse them with *aspirational* values. Aspirational values are what you want someday—they are a goal to achieve, not what your values are today. True CVs are beliefs you already have in yourself and your team, and they drive your actions.

To start the brainstorming process, think of your exemplary team members (this should include yourself). What are the qualities that stand out? Get input from some team members, but we do not recommend asking everyone on your team. There are likely some employees who do not reflect all your values and aren't team players. Asking for their input would not assist this process. Instead, talk to the key players on your team who have values you appreciate and celebrate—those team members you wish you could duplicate.

Core Values need to be authentic. Don't claim values that you aren't willing to hold yourself accountable to. This means a hard, long look in the mirror to see if you truly reflect these values. If the CVs are not meaningful, don't bother listing them.

Insincere or hollow words cause more harm than having none and may become a source

Core Values drive your actions.

of cynicism that will poison your culture. Choose Core Values that are impactful yet sincere.

Now that you have a list of words or attributes, you need to get specific. Think of the behaviors that support the value. Core Values shouldn't be a list of buzzwords. They need to encompass the daily actions of your team, including the Purpose of your company—the very core of your existence as a team. These are values/beliefs your team incorporates into all aspects of their work.

These three to ten clarified statements need to be owned by your entire team. This is what will attract and retain your team members … and deter those who don't share the same values. These values are not "permission to play" or minimum standards.

Make them easy to remember. Alliteration or an acronym can be helpful.

Brand Uniques—Your Unique Actions

Values + Action = Culture

Core Values + Brand Uniques = Culture

Your Brand Uniques are the unique actions your company takes to accomplish your important assignment—your Mission—because your Purpose matters. If you're following along, the CVs we just outlined plus our actions are what equals character and, collectively, culture. Many companies solve the same problems. So now, you're asking yourself why a client would want to work with you specifically. What do you do uniquely? Do you have a unique system for solving a problem?

List up to three BUs—unique actions—that your company performs every day to carry out your Mission.

Vision—Your Future

If you, as the leader, can't clearly communicate your Vision, how can you move toward it? How can you move your people toward it? A Vision is a clear statement of the result of your work. What does the future look like as a result of your Mission, Purpose, and Culture (CVs + BUs)?

Mission + Purpose + Culture = Vision

Your What + Your Why + Your How = Results

A commitment to Vision is where most people fail. If you can't sell yourself the Vision and commit to it, how are you going to sell anyone else your products or services? If you have a core product but constantly chase new ideas, is your core product really core? Your core product should fully support your Vision, and any new products should support it too.

Your team is an investment in your company, and you don't want to lose them because you can't see clearly where you're leading them. Leaders do not create confusion. Leaders lead. So, your Vision should be crystal clear, easily shared, and a filter for your everyday actions. Don't schedule another meeting if it doesn't align with your Vision. It should be that clear.

Make It Infinite

You want your company to outlast you. Your culture should too. Remember your infinity symbol; use the four keys below to ensure you don't get derailed.

1. Identify

Each of the five Company Core Components is crucial. You should have a short sentence that clearly communicates your Mission, Purpose, and Vision and a short list of CVs and BUs.

As we've mentioned in previous books in this series, you should also create your Vision Purpose Statement (VPS), which is a combination of the CCCs, along with some other key company focuses. If you haven't yet drafted yours, we've included a guide in the Toolbox.

2. Clarify

Don't rush finalizing your CCCs. Sleep on it and spend some time reflecting on them. Adjust as needed before moving on to implementation. Poor implementation of your CCCs will sour your culture. Don't claim components unless you are willing to execute them.

Newly defined CCCs need to be communicated to your team well, not just added to a page on your website. Develop a plan for how you will keep them at the forefront of team communication—beginning before the first interview and carried through to the last day of work.

3. Implement

Once you have these five components, start using them everywhere, both internally and externally. They should be in the Brand Guide your marketing team uses. You can include some of them in your email signature, website, social media profiles, et cetera. Look for ways to use your CCCs to enhance your marketing efforts. Your BUs should be used in all your marketing.

Your team needs to be reminded of the CCCs consistently. They need to be confident that there is no gap between what you're saying and what you're doing. Align your actions with your words. This will build a healthy culture of worth for your business.

Team satisfaction increases when they know what to expect and what metrics are used to measure success. Your Company Core Components, specifically the CVs, will do this for you. When sharing your CCCs, explain the CVs thoroughly—how they are used for evaluations, rewards, compensation, hiring, and firing.

4. Protect

Once you have established your CCCs, protect them. Protecting your core may include the following challenges:

- Firing a team member
- Having a difficult disciplinary conversation with an employee
- Not hiring a candidate who is incredibly skilled but lacks your values
- Passing on a business partnership with someone who doesn't share the same values
- Refusing to chase shiny objects and saying no to things that sound exciting but operate outside of your Purpose

Protecting your core takes commitment and discipline. It will be difficult at times.

Accountability isn't easy or for the faint of heart. Company Core Components leave executives open to criticism. They require leadership to be in touch with their team and receptive to feedback.

Company Core Components will keep you focused and hold you accountable to your Purpose—your reason for existing as a company. Protecting your CCCs will build a strong culture, resulting in a happy team that will be reflected in your bottom line.

If your Mission is to be carried out, your Company Core Components need to

- be clearly communicated.
- have strong boundaries.
- align with all projects, programs, and processes.
- be used as a filter for all new ideas, requests, and pursuits.

If at any time a new idea, client request, or new division doesn't align with your CCCs, you have to ask yourself, "Are we veering from our core? How is what we are doing positioning us in the marketplace?"

Use your CCCs to filter every shiny object that comes your way. You know one will. Quickly test it. Does it support your Purpose? Does it support your important assignment? Every new idea brought to the Leadership Team should be filtered through your CCCs, especially your Purpose. New products, new events, new ways to market … filter all of it. Will the new idea move you closer to your Vision or further from it?

Why It Matters

You may be leading your company, dreaming of starting one, or sitting on a team trying to find a way to successfully meet your goals. Whatever the situation, examine your behavior through the lens of your CCCs. It is not enough to create your CCCs and then leave them in your Team Handbook. You must identify and implement them with your team and clients. But most importantly, embody them as a company.

If what you say your company does, and the character in which you do it, doesn't align with your CCCs, there's a complex issue. Your team will see the disconnect. It will be difficult for your Sales Team to close a deal if they know what they are promoting to clients isn't actually happening in your company.

For example, you list a three-hour turnaround time as one of your BUs, but your team consistently fails to complete jobs in that timeframe. Your sales team will stop using this BU when selling. More importantly, they will feel like an imposter knowing that the final product or service isn't in alignment with that BU. This disconnect will affect your sales, your team, your culture, and ultimately your cash flow.

This applies to every component of your company but most importantly the Mission that inspired your team when you hired them. Your new hire bought into a Vision, likely when you or someone on your Leadership Team connected their role to the bigger picture. Once the big picture shifts, because your actions no longer align with the Company Core Components on paper, your team is left wondering how they fit into the new Vision they have yet to be shown.

It's not enough to conduct one meeting and announce a new change and expect everyone to fall in line. They need to see it.

They created a picture in their minds based on how the company was portrayed during the interview and onboarding processes. They sold themselves on the idea of working for your company. Maybe they've mapped out a plan in their

Remember the Mission that inspired your team.

minds of how they will move up in the ranks or someday retire from your company. They created a long-term plan and saw themselves as loyal employees. Now they feel disrespected, jaded, and unimportant. You've pulled the rug out from under the future they envisioned.

$$\ggg$$

After Brenda's first book, *Save the Butter Tubs!: Discover Your Worth in a Disposable World*, released in 2018, she was hired by her vanity publisher. Amanda started working for the same company about three months later. Because the work was remote, we didn't meet until a year later when we were assigned to room together at a business conference. Of course, we see it as a divine appointment now, but at the time, having never met, we weren't too excited about rooming with a stranger. We didn't realize it then, but we co-founded our company that weekend.

Immediately, we bonded over our critical thinking skills and strategic minds. Amanda began making lists, simplifying, and organizing, and Brenda did what comes naturally to her: solving problems, filling gaps, anticipating needs, and covering every detail to ensure the big picture came together better than planned.

Fast forward to March 13, 2020. Yep, the day toilet paper was flying off the shelves and the world was turning upside down. Brenda accepted the position of president of that same company during an organizational restructure. She worked alongside the company's visionary, and we operated on a unique entrepreneurial system in which her official title was "Integrator." That title suits Brenda 100 percent. Her passion for problem-solving and her ability to see situations in unique ways allow her to create simplified processes to help businesses thrive.

The same day, Amanda became the CFO and head of HR. Within four months of meeting, we were using our skills and talents in the C-Suite, working together daily to restructure the small business by creating and implementing systems and processes. As experts in simplification and solutions, we reworked programs to be profitable and more efficient, created new products to generate much-needed revenue for the company, and sought ways to add more joy to the daily functions, aligning the team in their grace-given gifts.

And yet, the more we worked with the company's visionary, the more we realized our Visions didn't align. After months of trying to keep the Mission intact, we could see that the original Vision we had both bought into no longer existed. All the hard work we had done to restructure the company was in vain. We began discussing our departures.

When the summer of 2021 rolled around, Brenda had a cancer scare that made her question, even more, why she was investing time following someone else's Vision that she didn't agree with. Then, as divinely as our first meeting, we both were awakened the same night with the same idea, even though we live 828 miles apart.

We began to plan our exits carefully, considering the team we would leave behind. Walking away from positions we once considered dream jobs wasn't something to take lightly. Walking away from the amazing clients was tough too. Walking away from our loyal team ... that was crushing.

So, why did we leave? The Mission—the important assignment. When we were hired, the company had a clear Mission that we both aligned with, and we even accepted certain promises based on our unique skills. Unfortunately, those promises were the result of people-pleasing. The visionary had no intention of following through. He was heading in a new direction, with no regard for how it affected the company or the team.

There were months of turmoil. We wanted to protect our team and wanted to do our job to correct the problems the company was experiencing.

The visionary wouldn't allow it, at one point declaring to the entire Leadership Team, "Get on board or get out."

Changing the Mission was a symptom of a bigger problem.

We walked, and like dominoes, many followed, including the entire Leadership Team.

Could this have been avoided? Could communication have been handled differently? In this particular situation, the company culture wasn't healthy. Changing the Mission was a symptom of a bigger problem. Instead of looking at the real issues and correcting them, the visionary tried to avoid them by going in another direction altogether.

As with anything, if you don't fix the root problems, you are destined to repeat them. If you are a people-pleaser or a micromanager, now is the time to quit those habits for a better Mission and a healthier culture. Take this time to examine your core and fix any root issues. Once your Company Core Components are in complete alignment—Mission + Purpose + Culture = Vision—share them everywhere and often.

Core Values + Brand Uniques = Culture

Mission + Purpose + Culture = Vision

Chapter Two

Derailment Proofing

Clients do not come first. Employees come first.
If you take care of your employees,
they will take care of the clients.

—Sir Richard Branson

You're the Boss. Act Like It.

We've heard it from more than one boss: "Don't call me the boss. We're all on the same team." If you've said it before, stop saying it now! To be the boss means you are the owner, and there's nothing wrong with that.

Yes, we want the team to take ownership, but they see you as their boss. You must learn to lead in a culture of worth. Stop playing small. Stop shirking responsibility. You are the boss because you are the owner of the company or responsible for a department. Your team needs your guidance. They need you to paint the Vision and show them the way to live out the Mission every day.

When bosses downplay their title, they aren't leading. This places the responsibility on the team and lets the boss off the hook.

Here's a fact: your team sees you as their boss. When you call unexpectedly, their first thought is "Oh, no! What did I do wrong?" It's like being

Stop playing small.

called to the principal's office. They will feel this way until you lead them well. Leading them well doesn't mean getting on their level. It means understanding their level and guiding them with clear communication and

Vision. Respect their position and the role they play in building your company and they will respect you as their boss.

Did you catch that? The way to gain respect from your team isn't by downplaying your rank and pretending you're on their level. It is by *caring* about them on their level. They know they aren't the boss, but they are smart, hardworking, creative, and innovative. You can either give them a seat at the table or watch them walk away while you pretend not to be their boss. Respect them and what they bring to the table. You need them. You hired them for a reason and invested time and money into them. Don't watch your investment walk out while you pretend not to be in charge.

Understand that your management and leadership styles have far-reaching implications. While you will have much to manage, remember that you don't manage people. You manage systems and processes, but you *lead* people.

Leaders must understand the mindset of those serving under them, who already feel vulnerable. We as leaders need to do everything in our power to make them feel valued and worthy in the workplace. By the very nature of leadership, those under you may feel intimidated, anxious, or even threatened by you. Remember, they interpret your leadership through the lens of their previous experiences.

If you've ever said, "At our company, we are like family," this will sting. A former colleague, Nathan Schock, shared this on LinkedIn, and he nailed it:

> CEOs, you have to STOP referring to your company as a family. It's unrealistic. Parents don't fire their children. Can you imagine?

Disowning your child for not meeting expectations.

"Mary, your mom and I discussed your position in the family, and we do not feel you are a good fit. Unfortunately, we will be letting you go and will need your last name back."

Mind-boggling, right? Now, do you see why it's not a good idea to call your team at work a family?

One commenter replied with another valid point that not all employees come from loving families. Calling your company a family could immediately send red flags or remind employees of an abusive situation. Stop trying to compare your company to something you can control and instead build a culture of worth.

When you clearly see the value of your employee, you understand the cost of retention. Your team is the engine of your company—the integral parts keeping your day-to-day operations running smoothly. They are on the front lines, dealing with client support and complaints. They are shielding you from thousands of tasks each day. Do you want to go back to doing those tasks? Do you want to answer every question or email complaint? We didn't think so. Value that front-line employee. They are a hero to both you and your client. Treat them as such.

Remember the Golden Rule—"Do unto others as you would have them do unto you?" This certainly applies to your clients. But in a way, your employee is also your client. You sold them on the job. They are paying you with their time and talent.

We can hear you questioning now, "But I pay them?" Yes, and when your client buys something with their money, you pay them with a product or service. It is an exchange. In the same way, you exchange a paycheck for your employee's time and attention.

Hopefully, you are providing more than a paycheck, or they will eventually leave. We will discuss compensation more in Chapter 6. For now, let's talk about some basic ways to gain their respect and create the culture of worth they are looking for.

1. Empower your employees.
2. Keep clear boundaries.
3. Give credit where credit is due.
4. Measure against your CVs.
5. Set an example.
6. Manage stress.
7. Give and receive feedback freely and respectfully.

Lead by example and the seven directives above will be amplified. This creates an environment where respect exists and is reciprocated.

Middle Management

There is a reason why it is called middle management. Middle managers are managing the expectations of both those above them and those below them on the OAR (Organization, Accountability, Responsibility) Chart (See Chapter 4 for a full explanation and how to use this chart). This may be you. If not, keep reading to understand the importance this layer of leadership has in any company. As leaders, you will be the bad guy at some point in your career, but you'll also grow through that experience.

Being in the middle can make you feel like a rubber band being pulled from both sides. You feel lonely because you aren't comfortable voicing concerns from below about your leaders *with* your leaders, and you certainly can't voice anything negative about your leaders to your subordinates.

While you're busy protecting those around you, people will talk behind your back. Not everyone will like your leadership style. Some people will leave. You'll have to make tough decisions, and you won't always get them right.

A culture of worth requires you to be transparent with those who lead you and with those whom you lead. Leaders should guide, praise, support, and most importantly, listen to what those they serve have to say. Why? Because as a leader in middle management, you buffer employees and clients from unnecessary communication, tasks, and decisions. Those above and below you should value and respect what you communicate.

If you don't feel comfortable talking openly with your leaders or those you lead, it's time to either shift the culture or shift your thoughts and realize why this communication is so valuable. Don't take things personally but do consider the feedback in whatever form it comes.

Be open to feedback from both sides. Ask for it. Learn from it. You will never stop learning. Communicate your needs and expectations to both sides clearly. As a leader in the middle, your role is to lead those under you, not above you. If those above you are consistently derailing your team by not following processes, micro-managing, and miscommunicating, it's time to set clear boundaries and protect your team. If you're the culprit, stop overstepping and support your middle management team. They are your Vision carriers.

Mismanagement

Micromanagement

If you want to grow your bottom line, you first have to grow people. Think of your team as a plant; if you overwater that plant, it will die. Or like that engine we mentioned earlier, don't flood your team. Throughout this book, we will discuss ways you communicate with your team. Veering outside of those parameters may be considered micromanaging.

At their core, people want to be validated. Paying your employees what they are worth is important, but this is only the foundation of respect.

Tapping into their expertise and using their grace-given gifts is what makes them feel **People want to be validated.** validated and fulfilled. Validation builds confidence. But so does letting your team fail. If you're micromanaging them, you are not letting them prove themselves or demonstrate their worth.

Don't be afraid to step back. Empower them. If your CCCs are clear, Job Descriptions accurate, and OAR Chart solid, then systems and processes (Standard Operating Procedures [SOP]) should be in place, and your team should be able to function without your direct oversight.

Control issues, such as asking to be copied on every email so that you can be kept in the loop, will derail your culture. This is common micromanaging. If you need to be kept in the loop, add the item to a meeting agenda or request a regular project update. You don't need the extra distraction of all those emails anyway.

If you set a project deadline with your team, communicate how you want to be updated along the way. This will keep you from checking in too often or not at all. Your intention is to help, but your team will most often feel smothered, untrusted, and devalued.

It's time to trust and empower your team with great tools, clear communication, working systems, and reasonable deadlines. Stop requiring approval on everything. Cast the Vision and set expectations but allow them to make their own mistakes. If you overstep or mismanage your team, you'll lose both clients and team members over time. Nothing says you lack value faster than a leader who oversteps. Will your team do things the way you want them done every time? Probably not. Will they make mistakes? Yes. Will they learn, grow, and become better employees? With your guidance, yes.

Boundaries

The boss is the boss, and the employee is the employee. As a leader, don't fall into the trap of thinking everyone on your team should be exactly like you. Respect each other's positions, personal time, processes, and responsibilities. Create a healthy, balanced working relationship.

As the boss, you are all in for your company, and while it's your desire that employees be all in as well, remember that they are an extension of you, but they are not you. They don't want to work 24/7, plus weekends, or skip vacations to build your company. They want respect, and they want to be valued for doing their job. Honoring their time and boundaries is important.

We can hear you now: "Well, they don't have to respond to the messages I send over the weekend. I just need to get the thoughts out of my head before I forget." Right, we understand. But you need to understand that as their boss, you have more influence than you realize. When you communicate with them in any way, they want to respond quickly. By communicating during their off time, you create unnecessary stress.

Boundaries are vital in all work situations. The introduction of work cellphones and other digital interoffice communication, and the lack of boundaries regarding their use, is the downfall of most workforces.

We do not own our employees and shouldn't expect them **Boundaries are vital in all work situations.** to be available 24/7. We've created an insecurity in our workforce in which taking a vacation or a sick day seems like a vulnerable request. This should not be the case!

Communicate through proper channels during regular business hours. Create a list of items you'll need to communicate during the next business day. Delegate the actual communication to your assistant if applicable. You can also schedule communication from most interoffice communication software. It is important to allow your team to rest and recuperate during their off time.

When executives and managers don't follow processes or miscommunicate, it breeds toxicity. We have seen toxicity move like a contagion across companies. And employees will leave. When leaders leave, the people under them sometimes follow suit.

Who's the Hero?

Make your team the heroes. Most CEOs and owners like to be the center of attention. But here's a secret: focus your attention on your team. If you make your team the clients' heroes, you will be your team's hero!

It's common marketing advice to make the client the hero. As your company grows, and you're distanced from the clients, don't lose sight of who your new clients are—your team. You can only shepherd the flock around you. Don't try to lead the entire company, the clients, your affiliates, et al. Your flock is your Leadership Team. This is who you should spend your time with and be pouring into, not running over. Then they will pour into their teams and their teams into your clients.

Building a culture of worth can save you valuable time and resources. Turnover costs your company greatly. Make your Leadership Team the heroes and teach them how to do the same with their teams. It starts with you.

Don't be intimidated by irreplaceable employees. These are the ones running circles around the others. Sometimes it may feel as though they are coming for your job. They are smart and have strengths you don't have. You need these people. Learn how to set your ego aside and collaborate with them. You will go further faster.

If someone is irreplaceable, treat them as such. If you can't find a way to collaborate, they will take their expertise elsewhere.

These employees like a good challenge but demand the respect their skills deserve. Look

Set aside ego and collaborate.

for and validate growers if you want to grow.

You hired people based on the strengths they bring. Now let them use those strengths. The minute someone feels stifled, they start looking elsewhere.

Trust and vulnerability go a long way in a culture of worth. Some leaders see vulnerability as a weakness or use it to manipulate. If this describes you, take a step back and start building trust. If someone chooses to be vulnerable with you by sharing something personal or different, this isn't a weakness but bravery. They are saying they trust you.

In turn, be sure you can trust the people you choose to be vulnerable with. Let them know that you are being vulnerable, especially if it is something you want kept confidential.

In a former position in which Brenda served as integrator to a visionary, she often felt vulnerable sharing her ideas. There were times the visionary would sternly remind her that he was the visionary and that she should keep her ideas to herself. Other times, he would take her ideas and present them as his own. Both behaviors came out of his own insecurities as a leader, and neither left Brenda feeling like the hero. His desire to be the hero ruined the relationship and trust.

When others are vulnerable with you, thank them and acknowledge their vulnerability. Let them know the boundaries in which the information will be shared or used, if applicable.

Never take your employees' ideas as your own. Give credit where credit is due. Let them shine in the areas of their grace-given gifts. It's why you hired them. Don't manipulate others with false vulnerability or self-deprecation but do stay humble. The best superheroes know how to disguise themselves.

The Difficult Ones

You'll have some shining stars to keep happy, challenged, and feeling valued, and then you'll have some difficult employees too. Even the best hires can become difficult as circumstances change. Find the root of the toxicity. One toxic employee can turn the workplace culture upside down quickly.

Even if they haven't broken a policy, you may need to discuss how they are failing to meet the Core Values. Are they an asset to your team? Keep them if they are willing to change their behavior. Are they replaceable? Make a change. If you want to keep them, get to the root of the issue. Is their commute causing them to be late or grumpy? Could you change their work environment? Can they work remotely? Maybe they are constantly missing their children's important events and feel guilty; maybe balancing their personal life and work has become impossible with their schedule. Can you change their work schedule? This could be an easy solution if you have the flexibility. Anticipating needs is not just for your clients' sake but for your employees too.

As with all communication, timing is everything. And remember, **actions are communication**. If your difficult employee is always late to your weekly meetings, their lateness is telling you something. Maybe their timing is off. Maybe they aren't managing their time well, and they scheduled another meeting too close to this one. Or maybe you send the information for the meeting too late, and they have to hustle to review it before they attend. Every problem has a root, and every problem has a solution. Find both.

Quickly get to the root issue. Don't let problems fester. Anticipate the needs of your employees. Make the necessary changes before issues affect culture.

Emotion Management

As mentioned earlier, your team is comprised of emotional beings. Including you. While you can't manage the emotions of others, you can set an example. Start by creating an environment that lives up to your CVs and Purpose. Manage your emotions when interacting with your peers and lead with emotional intelligence as well.

Emotional intelligence may be a new concept for you. Most employers are concerned with intelligence and skill but never consider the emotional aspect.

If you work in HR or upper management, you will likely at some point in your career have to fire someone. If you aren't emotionally intelligent enough to handle the responsibility, you aren't fit for the role. When you fire someone, there will be emotions. They may cry, scream, or accuse you of anything from discrimination to abuse. We've seen leaders emotionally unequipped to handle these situations try to rehire people who have quit or fire people via email to avoid emotions. Neither is a professional or intelligent way to conduct business. Negotiating someone's tenure is very different from rehiring someone who quits. Know the difference and respond accordingly.

In Brenda's first book, she states,

> "Maturity isn't about age, it's about responsibility."

You have to be emotionally mature enough to handle the responsibility. We have seen example upon example in which both employee and employer haven't possessed the emotional intelligence or capacity for their position. This doesn't mean you don't ever show emotion. Emotional intelligence is showing the proper emotions at the appropriate times. Be aware of your emotions when responding to emails, clients' requests, negative feedback, et cetera. Be sure you are responding professionally and not reacting out of emotion.

Your employees will be most productive when working in their grace-given gifts. Create a space where they are free to operate as themselves without minimizing them, ignoring them, or flying off the handle. It can be risky to expose yourself in a way that may not affect positive consequences. In this way, the biggest barrier to self-expression is an unhealthy workplace culture. Remember the children joyfully pursuing their purpose at the beginning of the book? Think about how freely children express themselves. To allow creativity to flow, you must allow expression and learn to manage your emotional responses.

Leaders should avoid creating situations in which their team feels vulnerable. This is where vulnerability and abuse intersect. It's one thing if an employee chooses to be vulnerable with you, but making them feel vulnerable is unhealthy. Creating a healthy culture *allows* for vulnerability. An unhealthy culture can *force* vulnerability.

Don't ask personal questions if you aren't emotionally equipped to handle the answers. If you are trying to create a culture of worth by investing in your team's personal lives, but you can't emotionally handle what they are doing outside of work, you are going about this the wrong way. Some companies use "Personal Best/Business Best" as an icebreaker. While this can help you get to know your team on a deeper level, if you ever take something that was said and use it against them or to control them, you are opening yourself and your company to liability. Your team has a personal life, and it will affect their work from time to time. Handle this information with care.

Before you start sharing personal information or new ideas, you need to understand what is and isn't appropriate to share and *when* it is appropriate to share. If you are sharing your vulnerabilities at every turn, you'll be seen as not only weak but as a victim.

Manage expectations: both your expectations and those of your team. Create a safe environment for self-expression. Don't take things personally when others share. Don't react. Take time to respond thoughtfully.

Stress Management

When people are stressed, they are often distracted. We see this frequently when people aren't actively listening. When someone shares something personal, possibly heartbreaking, and your response is "Cool," and then you move on to your agenda … this is not healthy. As a leader, you must actively listen. Set aside whatever is stressing you at the moment, and be fully present with your team and your clients.

Don't expect your employees to keep their personal business at home. People will carry their experiences with them. While they can (and should) leave the drama at home, don't expect them to not be affected by their personal lives. Examples of circumstances to be aware of might be someone caregiving for an elderly parent or a newborn, a family member in the hospital, or a recent diagnosis.

Prepare to handle these situations by talking with your Leadership Team ahead of time. Some ways to show support can be to adjust workloads, allow time off when needed, or send a card or gift to acknowledge the situation. You can use information provided on the employee's Fun Fact Form (included in the Toolbox) to personalize the gift.

While you can't manage the stress in your team's personal lives, you can manage how you contribute to it. Manage your stress. Stress leaks and flows to your team. When stress is managed, it's easier to make decisions and solve problems. You cannot be the leader your team needs if you are not in control of yourself.

Stress management includes the following:

- Flexibility—Adapt emotions, thoughts, and behaviors.
- Tolerance—Cope with stressful situations.
- Optimism—Maintain a positive attitude and outlook on work and life.
- Outlets—Provide a way for people to communicate when they are feeling stressed.
- Anticipation—Be prepared. Life happens.

Regardless of the position—boss, middle management, front line employee, et al—you hold within the company, keeping stress at bay will create a better environment for everyone. Respecting the positions and the roles each plays within the company is key to derailment proofing your culture.

Chapter Three

Legit or Quit

You don't build business, you build people,
then people build business.

—Zig Ziglar

You're either in business or you have a hobby.
If you are in business, you have to follow
the standards and meet expectations, or your
team and clients won't take you seriously. You
could also wind up paying some hefty penalty
fees or lose your business altogether. If you're
not willing to comply, you should rethink your
business.

Expected Standards

With the ease at which employees find and share information, it is imperative that you maintain corporate standards at your company or your team will be employed elsewhere.

Clients expect standards as well, and when those aren't met, it is embarrassing and detrimental to your team. Simple, easily overlooked details, like broken links on your website or social media accounts, give your client a reason to look elsewhere. Even little mistakes create additional work for your customer support team. Cover your basics.

If quality control is a recurring issue in your company, it is time to make it a priority. Hire a consultant or dedicated team member to confirm your company is meeting standard expectations across the board. Some of these items include benefits, safety, compliance, training, privacy, and delivery of products or services.

One of the best tools you can use to achieve quality outcomes consistently is a well-documented Standing Operating Procedure (SOP). Throughout this book, we refer to processes. Any process you repeat should be documented as an SOP. The SOP should include clear-cut instructions and, if applicable, step-by-step directions. These should be kept digitally and easily accessible to the employees who will utilize them. Many of the tools we've made available can become part of your SOPs. Some companies simply call SOPs their process docs. Regardless of what you title them, having them in place will

- save time in training.
- maintain quality.
- reduce miscommunication.
- guide accountability.
- eliminate unnecessary steps.

At a minimum, each of your departments should have SOPs in place for their over-arching functions.

Train and Cross-Train

One benefit, to both the employee and the company, often overlooked is training. Your team should be properly trained on the best equipment you can afford to accomplish the job.

Build confidence among team members with the proper training and equipment. They will perform better when they feel well-equipped to do their job. Outdated and broken equipment can be costly in both time and potential safety incidents. If your software is outdated, or you don't have the correct software for a task, it slows down productivity. Employees will lose respect for you, your company, and their position. Provide ongoing training if the roles require it. If you want your employees to stay sharp, provide them with the tools and training they need and also provide the time to learn.

Cross-training is also often overlooked due to time and other constraints, but it will add value to your team as well as your company. Cross-training is a valuable benefit to an employee. Your employee started their job with a certain skill set; by cross-training them, you are educating them and furthering their professional development. When you cross-train your employees, you open lines of communication and collaboration. If you silo your employees, the growth is limited to one person's ability to think bigger. But cross-training can expedite growth.

Having your team cross-trained will save you time and money if someone is out sick, leaves suddenly, promotes out of their role, or unexpectedly retires. Why an employee leaves a position is irrelevant. You should have someone who can step in, even if it is only for a brief period. If you are a small business, cross-training your employees may be the only way your business can continue to function if someone is on vacation. You can't afford to wait for key players to return if their day-to-day responsibilities affect your output.

If you only have one person responding to customer service emails and that person goes on vacation, who handles their inbox? You? Nope. Just let the emails pile up and expect the employee to do double the work when they return? No. Cross-train someone whose role interacts with the same processes or people. The training time will be shorter and more productive. Every position in your organization should be cross-trained or, at the very least, backed up by someone else.

Safety and Compliance

The integrity of your company is on the line when it comes to safety and compliance, regardless of your industry or the size of your team. Regulations and legalities can be overlooked at times, especially as small businesses grow, because they require time, money, and other resources. Slow down long enough to consult with a legal professional when needed. There are obvious legal reasons why you should make certain your company is providing a safe work environment and is compliant in all the necessary ways, but this is also essential for employee retention.

Here are a few questions to ask yourself:

- Does your company have all the required licenses, registrations, and permits?
- Are you following all safety standards that apply to your business?
- Are you in compliance with Department of Labor standards or state-specific standards?
- Do all your team members have the correct employment classification (exempt

versus non-exempt, contractor versus employee)?

• In the event of an accident, are you and your employees protected and covered by insurance?

• Are all appropriate federal, state, and local taxes being paid (payroll, sales tax, etc.)?

• Have you conducted the necessary background checks on employees who require it for their position?

When employees see that you are cutting corners, ignoring regulations, or evading compliance, it leads them to question the security of the company and their jobs. If employees are asked to intentionally go against standards or regulations, they will question the integrity of the business and wonder if they are willing to risk their own reputation. Odds are they won't be and will find an employer who doesn't create this type of dilemma.

Don't neglect the basic need for safety. Your employees need to feel secure while working for you. Overlooking this need can be detrimental to culture and increase employee turnover. Compliance benefits both you, as the employer, and your team. The more protected your team feels, the more likely they are to work hard and be committed to your company.

Providing the correct safety training shows value to the employee, as well as respect for the tools and equipment you've provided them. Leading by example is the best practice. It could be something as simple as locking up the building at the end of the day, closing the blinds so people outside can't see your valuable equipment, or setting the alarm. The size of your business and your team will determine who is responsible for these tasks.

Structure It

Back to the differentiator shared at the beginning of this chapter—business or hobby? The goal of a business is to make money while solving a problem for your client. You can't be a legitimate business without properly setting up, tracking, and responsibly managing the company finances.

This high-level view of finances is addressed in this chapter because it is important to the legitimacy of your business. If you aren't confident in your skills when it comes to finances, hire a consultant immediately—even before you hire someone internally. This will help you understand what your business actually needs when hiring for a financial position. Depending on the size of your business, this may be an internal role or an outside consultant.

Do you need a certified public accountant, a bookkeeper, or a chief financial officer? Skill level and experience are critical when it comes to finances. The wrong hire in this position could sink your ship. Once you have the correct finance team in place, work with your professional to set up your financial systems. These systems should include checks and balances to ensure there is the appropriate oversight on expenses, investments, deposits, and handling of cash.

One of the most common issues with small business finances is the lack of an approval process for expenses. As your team grows, decide early on who approves purchases and if employees will have access to a company credit card. If employees are expected to make certain purchases on their own and then submit requests for reimbursement, ensure that the process is respectful and timely. Don't expect employees to regularly make large purchases and then not reimburse them until the end of the month. This can cause undue stress to their personal financial situation.

Financial Reports

Regularly review your company's basic financial reports. These should include the profit and loss statement (P&L), balance sheet, cash flow statement, accounts receivable and payable (AR/AP), and budgets. Reviewing your finances will assist with identifying trends that will help you make better financial decisions and address issues before they get out of control. Understanding the financials will also allow you to gauge when and how to better compensate your employees.

Don't review these reports alone. Share them with your Leadership Team. Discuss areas of concern. Strategize how to cut expenses and be more profitable. To succeed in business and build a healthy culture, you have to get comfortable talking about money with your leaders. Create an environment that allows for open and honest communication.

Responsibility

Make wise decisions with the company money. Your team sees how you spend it, and this will greatly impact whether they feel valued by the company.

We once had a company suggest a retreat for some of its remote employees. When we saw who was on the list to attend, we were shocked. This included employees who only worked ten hours per month in non-revenue generating positions while excluding others who were making huge impacts on the company's bottom line. All employees are valuable, but you must be selective about who you are whisking away for retreats or rewarding with other benefits.

Finances are facts, and numbers don't lie. As difficult as it can be to see at times, you can't make company-wide decisions about how to move forward if you don't know where you are moving forward from.

As technology advances and remote work becomes more accessible, candidates seeking employment have greater options and can be more selective about what they want—and don't want—from the company they work for, including benefits. Offer what you can within your budget. If you need ideas, we discuss some in Chapter 6 and offer additional ideas in *The Onboarding Process*.

Finances, legalities, compliance, and standards can be challenging for small businesses, but all of these support your credibility and integrity. Invest the effort to set up the necessary processes and exceed standards. This will go a long way when it comes to retaining the best employees for your company.

Chapter Four

Accountability

*Everyone talks about building
a relationship with your customers.
I think you build one with your employees first.*

—Angela Ahrendts

Chart It

If you're the owner/founder/CEO, it isn't expected for you to communicate with your entire company on a regular basis. Depending on the size of your company, you may not even know all your employees by name. This is why an OAR Chart—seeing the **organization** of your company employees at-a-glance, knowing who holds whom **accountable**, and what each individual is **responsible** for—is necessary.

Is your inner circle clearly identified within your organization? This is your flock. Regardless of what you call them—C-Suite, Executive Team, or Leadership Team—you should only be interacting with three to seven leaders on a regular basis. Those leaders will work with the leaders under them, and those will work with the next level of employees, and so forth.

If you are just starting a company, your team may be comprised of only three to seven people. This does not imply that each of them should have a seat on your Leadership Team. Leadership positions require qualified leaders and not just tenured employees.

If you haven't created an OAR Chart for your company, now is the time. Some companies refer to it as an organization or accountability chart. We take it one step further by adding responsibilities.

Brenda is a United States Air Force veteran, and this type of chart is a no-brainer for her. But while serving under someone much less experienced in the workforce, she quickly realized that not everyone understands the flow of an OAR Chart, regardless of its title. We've seen charts that included only two boxes for more than thirty employees. The two leaders of the company and their assistants were in one box at the top of the chart with a line connecting below to another box with the rest of the employees' names. It was no wonder there was absolutely zero accountability! No one knew what other people in the company did, much less who reported to whom.

Your chart's organization should reflect who is accountable to whom. An OAR Chart will include a box for each role in the company. That box should include the title of the role, the person or people filling that role, and the key responsibilities of the role. It should link directly to the one person who holds that role accountable to their goals and productivity.

You don't need separate boxes if multiple people share the same role. For example, if you have several Customer Service Representatives, and they all report to the same person, set up one box with all the names. If one of those representatives is a lead, and others report to them, the lead role has its own box on the chart. Connect another box below it with the names of the direct reports. See example here:

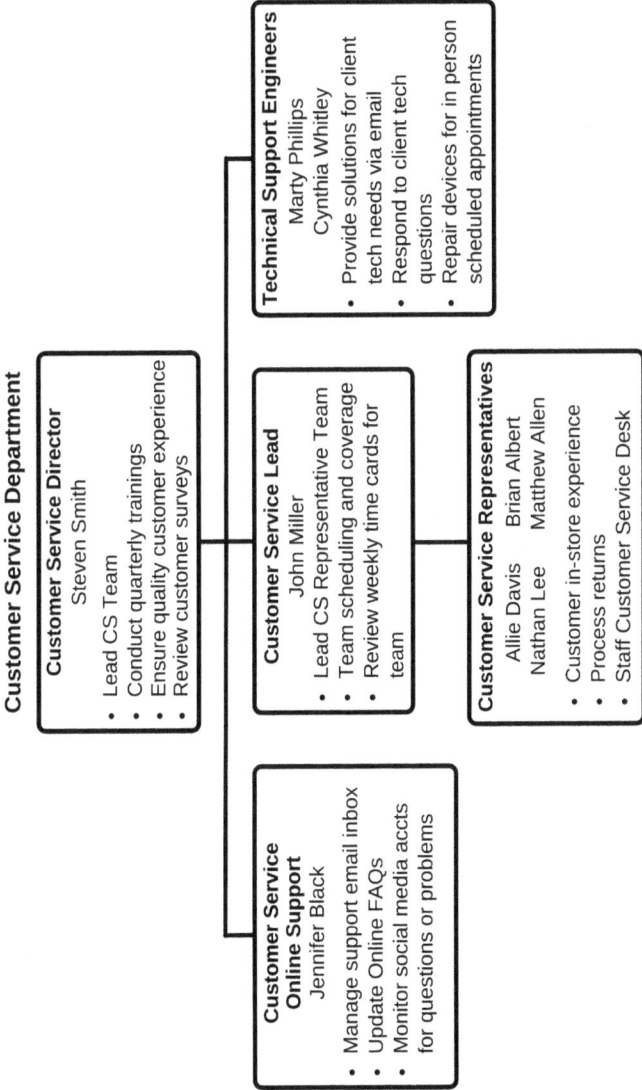

Customer Service Department

Customer Service Director
Steven Smith
- Lead CS Team
- Conduct quarterly trainings
- Ensure quality customer experience
- Review customer surveys

Technical Support Engineers
Marty Phillips
Cynthia Whitley
- Provide solutions for client tech needs via email
- Respond to client tech questions
- Repair devices for in person scheduled appointments

Customer Service Lead
John Miller
- Lead CS Representative Team
- Team scheduling and coverage
- Review weekly time cards for team

Customer Service Representatives
Allie Davis   Brian Albert
Nathan Lee   Matthew Allen
- Customer in-store experience
- Process returns
- Staff Customer Service Desk

Customer Service Online Support
Jennifer Black
- Manage support email inbox
- Update Online FAQs
- Monitor social media accts for questions or problems

If you don't have this kind of structure in your company and need support in creating it, reach out to us for help. When you can reference one chart and know who in your company is responsible for what, you can identify issues, clearly see who is leading the way, and spot any gaps.

Thus, your OAR Chart should clearly define who does what. Clear Job Descriptions set expectations. Clear expectations go a long way in retaining your team.

In *The Hiring Process*, we suggest giving titles "that edify—titles your team will be proud to display beside their names." Titles matter. Give your employee a title that not only edifies them but also adds clarity about their role for your company. Respect the position and the person who fills it.

When setting up your OAR Chart, you may realize that there are more roles that need to be filled than qualified people. If this is the case, the first thing to do is a Capacity Check. We explain this in Chapter 5 and provide an example in the Toolbox.

Once you have your OAR Chart completed and have filled any open roles internally, you can review *The Hiring Process* and draft Job Descriptions for any open positions.

Before filling any role on your OAR Chart, please review the following dos and don'ts:

Don't

1. Bring in outside people for an inside job.
2. Hire unqualified people.
3. Allow people to stay who poison your culture.
4. Allow multiple people to fill a role that should be filled by one individual.
5. Assign too many direct reports to one leader.

Do

1. Consider the person's capabilities, including emotional capability.
2. Use the Interview ScoreCARD (from *The Hiring Process* Toolbox) to ensure fit.
3. Group similar processes together under one leader.
4. Represent roles in the C-Suite or Leadership Team correctly.

After creating your OAR Chart, make it available to the entire company. Keeping it as a digital, living document will save time and expedite the process of revisions. As we discussed in *The Onboarding Process,* your OAR Chart is a critical tool for connecting and communicating.

Own Your Mistakes

If you're not willing to be held accountable as a leader, how can you expect accountability from your employees? A large part of being an entrepreneur or CEO is ownership—owning not only your company and its successes but the mistakes as well. Acknowledge any mistakes you make, take steps to correct them, and try to avoid them in the future. Accountability can be humbling, but in order to protect company culture, it is a necessity.

Accountability to your Company Core Components is crucial. You laid the foundation with your Mission and Purpose, and now everyone in the organization should be held accountable to them, including you. Impulse control as a CEO, visionary, or leader can sometimes be hard. We are all learners. We like new information, and sometimes new information leads to new ideas, but these should serve the big picture.

If you're constantly pursuing something shiny and new, you're wasting valuable resources of time, energy, and money, and you may possibly be ruining your company culture.

Remember to assess each new idea, using your Vision as a filter. Some ideas will be worth the effort; others will be cut quickly. Some ideas may be good, but the timing isn't right. Don't toss the ideas in the trash. Capture them in a file or list to be revisited and possibly implemented when the timing is better.

Many people are addicted to being busy. Busyness has become an expectation. Ask anyone how they are, and you'll likely hear "Busy." As Brenda says in her first book,

> "It's not about being busy, but being fruitful."

Maybe fruitful doesn't resonate with you, but as a business owner, productivity does. If your team is always busy but never productive, you have a serious issue.

The same goes for you as a leader. If you are the visionary of a company, you can't fulfill your role if you leave no time to create the Vision. Invest in yourself and your fellow leaders. Admit that you don't have all the answers and work to better yourself. Join a mastermind program, read books that teach you better strategies (like this one), or hire a coach or consultant.

Lastly, when it comes to mistakes, don't give your team "boss" responsibilities unless you're also giving them the "boss" paycheck and title. This mistake tends to creep up. As you work alongside someone, it's natural that they learn from you. Maybe they've always been capable in their role, but now you see them performing at a higher degree. You started by giving them small tasks, which over time, morphed into a level of new responsibility that exceeds their compensation. At first, they take on the additional responsibility in hopes of recognition or perhaps simply because they are capable. Over time, however, resentment will build.

Promote and pay people what they are worth before it is too late. Take into consideration the cost of replacing them and the investment of time and resources you've already made. The longer your employees stay with your company, the more experienced they become with your systems, products, clients, and fellow team members. Your team is a valuable asset you want to hold on to. Treat them as such from the start, and you'll be creating a culture of worth.

Own Your Numbers

Don't ignore numbers—budgets, financial reports, sales metrics, marketing ROI, and so on. We discussed finances in the last chapter, and it is worth repeating. Share the numbers (the good and the bad) with your leadership. Tracking metrics across your company is a must. You can't measure what you don't track, just like you won't know you're winning if you don't keep score.

If you've ever tried to lose weight, you know it's just as important to track your body measurements as it is to watch the scale. You may also be counting calories or looking at health metrics like blood pressure and cholesterol. Tracking the various metrics associated with a goal is important because they reflect different parts of the process. By tracking metrics, you show your team that you are a legitimate business looking for real results.

Track metrics in each department to determine the health of the department at a glance. Don't track numbers just for the sake of tracking something. Which numbers measure the health of the processes you have in place and directly affect the bottom line? Those are the numbers to track. This shouldn't be complicated. Being accountable to the numbers shows progress toward the company goals. When numbers are off track, stop and assess the situation. Don't keep moving forward without understanding how they went off track and how to course-correct.

Own Your Goals

The goals you set for yourself daily may be aggressive, but continuing to set aggressive goals for your team isn't healthy. Goals need to be realistic and attainable. Goals should be set *with* your team, not *for* them. We've seen large companies set goals based on their desires from a corporate seat miles away from the daily working environment. Often those setting these goals are separated by multiple levels of management from those expected to achieve the goals.

If communication is good and culture is healthy, these goals are usually realistic. When there is miscommunication, goals can become misaligned. For example, say your large company continues to set sales goals based on previous growth and sales metrics. If, however, one of your major clients awards your contract to another company, yours won't stand a chance at hitting its sales goal. The entire process needs to be evaluated when setting goals. In this case, the new goal could be to contract with another major client. Depending on the size of the new client's need, your sales goal should be adjusted.

If you have personal goals or responsibilities within the company as its leader, be sure to lead by example. Shrugging off your responsibilities by missing deadlines, showing up to meetings unprepared or late, or changing goals midstream to avoid failure are all surefire ways to lose your team's respect. You wouldn't tolerate this kind of behavior from them, so why would you set this example?

When setting company goals, it's important for the leadership of the company to show ownership. What part of the goal will you support? Maybe you're not the one responsible for the sales, but are you the one responsible for negotiating vendor contracts? Are you responsible for providing the necessary training?

Part of goal-setting and accomplishing goals successfully is anticipating the needs. Looking at all that must come together to ensure a successful outcome will help you avoid mistakes that could cost you time, money, clients, employees, and a shift in your culture.

If your goal is to close **Anticipate** fifty new deals this month, **needs.** but your infrastructure can't support that goal, you're going to end up with a culture of panic, not a culture of worth.

Two more wise reasons to anticipate needs are that you'll (1) start to see patterns emerge and (2) be able to project future products, growth opportunities, and hiring needs. Essentially, anticipating needs is getting ahead of the game.

When setting goals, you'll want to consider those that motivate your team and/or clients. Both like to be involved in exciting growth. Are your goals exciting? Are they forward-thinking? If your goal is just to keep your doors open, take a closer look at your culture and ask yourself what is derailing it. Go back to the Workplace Culture Assessment in the Toolbox. If you didn't take it, do so now. You must discover the root problem with your culture, otherwise, your goals will always be out of reach.

Refer to your Company Core Components. If you and your team are having to work outside of your sweet spot (beyond your BUs) on a regular basis, you need to realign your CCCs. It's important when goal-setting to know how much of a workload you and your team can handle. Your goals should be a direct reflection of your Mission and capacity. What is your important assignment, and what are you doing every day to make that happen? If your goals don't support the Mission, your company will eventually implode. Remember, values plus action equal culture. If your CCCs say one thing but your goals and actions to achieve those goals say another, your culture will be unhealthy.

Use the Goal MAP from the Toolbox to map your individual goals, aligning them with your CCCs. This tool was introduced in *The Onboarding Process* Toolbox for your new hire to use, but it should be used with every goal moving forward in the company. This tool will help you identify the resources needed to accomplish your goal and outline the process that leads to its accomplishment. As you'll read in Chapter 5, you should review current Goal MAPs with your employees during quarterly and annual meetings. If your employees are setting goals as part of the bigger company goal, they should each have a Goal MAP completed.

As you can see, accountability plays an integral role in reaching your goals. It's important to keep everyone rowing in the same direction. The result will be accomplished goals. Accomplishments validate effort, which creates a fulfilled team. A fulfilled team perseveres. Having a solid integrator on your team is essential for breaking down goals and exploring who will accomplish these goals. If you don't have an integrator on your team, consider bringing in a consultant or, if applicable, hire one internally.

Goal MAP

Goal State in one sentence or word that will be easily recognized on the calendar by all involved in the completion of it.

Due Date
6/30

Create and roll-out company-wide Team Calendar

What problem does it solve? Frequent confusion regarding the timing and location of important meetings. Absenteeism and tardiness. Overbooked calendars. Questions about company holidays.

What solution does it provide? Accurate information in a centralized location.

Coordinates How is this moving you in the direction of the company Vision?
The calendar will assist with important company-wide information being communicated

Measurable (quantity, results, deadline)
Team Calendar created, including all company holidays and meetings and shared to team by June 30.

Accomplished with
(supplies, software, tools OR people via delegation, coordination, or input)

G-suite calendar
Integrator
HR
Tech

Process to completion	Due Dates
Break your goal into milestones	
Step 1 Confirm holidays & meetings with HR	4/15
Step 2 Input all dates, times, and locations into calendar.	4/28
Step 3 Coordinate with tech to ensure everyone has access.	5/10
Step 4 Create "how-to access" screencast & FAQ doc.	5/22
Step 5 Develop rollout plan with Integrator.	6/1
Final Review Submit for Leadership Team review and approval	6/15
Describe what complete looks like	
"How-to access" screencast & FAQs shared with the team.	
Team Calendar is in use & accessible by all employees.	

Add milestone dates to your calendar and anyone else's working with you on this goal.

Chapter Five

Operational Communication

*If you're good to your staff when things are
going well, they'll rally when times go bad.*

—Mary Kay Ash

Clear communication is key to successful
relationships and business operations. Good
communication conveys worth and value.
As we discussed in *The Hiring Process*
and *The Onboarding Process*, communication
is the consistent theme when you work
with people. Whether with your team,
clients, or vendors, if you learn how to

communicate well, you will build strong, long-term relationships.

Just as *not* making a decision *is* actually making a decision, *not* communicating *is* communicating. Inaction speaks as loudly as action. What are your actions (or inaction) saying to your team? Poor communication sends a clear message that you don't value them.

Here are ways you communicate with your company that you may or may not be aware of. Review and make notes where there is room for improvement.

Email

Email should primarily be used for external communications. Set company boundaries and guidelines for expected response time. The response time should be in direct relation to the products and services you deliver. No one in your company should be distracted by email notifications buzzing incessantly all day, unless their specific role is customer service email response. But even then, set clear office hours for the role, especially if they work remotely.

In general, expectations on checking email should be limited to a few times per day. This will increase productivity and limit distractions. You need to be agreeable with this schedule across the board, and you should be, given the other ways you can communicate with your team, which we will discuss next.

If you are copied on an email, don't reply unless you were asked to. Being copied just means the sender wants you to see it, not respond or take action. Never email tasks. Assign tasks in your appropriate project management software. The only emails you send internally should be those external emails you need to forward to the appropriate team member.

Internal Communication Platform

Internal communication platforms are designed for simple communication, quick questions, alerts, and team announcements outside of meetings. If you read *The Onboarding Process*, this story will be familiar:

We once worked with a small business that purchased a communication platform for their team. It was greatly needed to improve team communication. However, the leadership didn't take the time to define and share best practices with their team. This platform had the ability to post content that would distribute to every person in the company and individually notify them. One team member would repeatedly ask questions on the platform that should have been directed to a single person rather than the entire company. We liken her poor etiquette to a school building where someone continually uses the loudspeaker to broadcast their questions to every classroom instead of contacting a specific teacher.

This behavior caused several problems:

1. It created a company-wide distraction. Think about the time lost when this happened on a regular basis.

2. The team member with the answer would reply on the same inappropriate platform. Thus, the company-wide distraction continued.

3. These distractions led to frustration among team members. Those who better understood how to use the platform would complain to others, "Why doesn't she just ask one person her questions?" Hence more distractions and lost time.

4. This bad habit was then replicated by other team members and new hires. "I see that she asks all of her questions here. I guess that's what I'm supposed to do too."

5. When too many distractions like this occur, it becomes noise, and your team will be conditioned to tune out valuable information.

Allowing this to get out of hand is harmful to company culture as it appears no one is in charge and correcting this poor behavior. Address such situations quickly. Privately let the offender know the appropriate way to use the software. This may include walking her through the proper steps or directing her to a training video. Remove the content from the wrong place so others don't feel obligated to respond and thereby put an end to the distractions.

Another issue with multiple internal communication platforms is when team members don't understand which one to use. Perhaps they send the same message across all platforms and disrupt the workflow multiple times. The result is confusion about where to send the answer. This is especially harmful if done by your Leadership Team. They can open the door for bad habits to spread. As they lead, others will follow.

While one incident may seem insignificant, if continued, it has a snowball effect that leads to more wasted time and a lack of efficiency. This can have a negative impact on your company's culture. Culture affects your productivity. Productivity affects your bottom line. Little things matter.

Learn how to properly use your internal communication platform and make sure your team follows suit.

Project Management Software

Commitment and consistency are requird for systems and processes to be successful. Introducing project management software can be a game-changer for small to medium-sized businesses. They are worth the investment if properly implemented. We have seen too many times when small businesses purchase software, attempt to set it up, and then go back to their old ways. Do your research to find the software that fulfills your task or project management needs, then commit to using it. Assign a team member to take ownership of the project management software, learn all its capabilities, and train the rest of the team.

If you have email, an internal communication platform, and project management software, understand which is the best method for different types of communication. Follow the processes your team already has in place for communication systems. If these systems aren't working for you, fix them, because working outside of them creates chaos.

Talk to your Leadership Team if you aren't aware of the system you need. Most companies are underutilizing the project management systems they've paid for. You may already have a solution available. Connect with the team member assigned to oversee and train on the software and let them know what you need.

If your systems aren't working for you, you need to ask yourself, "Is it working for the team and the clients?" If so, you may need to learn more about how the system functions and how to best utilize it. If it is not working for your team or your clients, it's time to make a change.

The basic operations of your company should each have a clear system (documented in an SOP) with a system owner. The system owner should be included as part of the person's role on the company OAR Chart from Chapter 4. This communicates to your entire team who is in charge of implementing the system. Knowing who owns what system is important as your team expands.

Systems increase productivity and save time and resources. You may not have software in place yet to support these systems, but as you grow, you'll know when the time is right to upgrade to specific project management software. We encourage you to allow the infrastructure of your operations to be built early with a solid foundation that will support your developing business.

Meetings

Meetings should be kept to a minimum but should occur regularly as a part of your company operations. Meetings exist to discuss issues, ideas, upcoming events, and strategies to better the company or department. Always be fully present when meeting with your team. Their time is valuable, what they have to say is important, and how you listen during a meeting will communicate this to them. Remember, your team members are valuable assets that you've invested in.

Always set a meeting agenda, and be clear on the meeting's goal before scheduling. This should be a Standard Operating Procedure for your team. Never walk into a meeting that doesn't have an agenda and don't expect your team to either. Remember that unnerving principal's office feeling? That's what it feels like to walk into a meeting not knowing the goal or the agenda. A clear meeting agenda sets boundaries, allows attendees to come prepared, and ensures that you aren't rehashing the same topics from meeting to meeting.

It is common courtesy to include in the agenda the team members, clients, or guests who will be present at the meeting. Not including key players in important meetings—or including the wrong players altogether—can wreck your culture. If you invite subordinates to a meeting without their leader, what message are you sending that leader? The last thing you want is to create confusion by including someone in a meeting who normally wouldn't attend. Avoid the drama; if you intend to include someone new in a meeting, add their name to the agenda with a brief explanation.

For example: "Susie will be joining us today for the leadership meeting. I've asked her to present an idea that I think will benefit the company, and I look forward to your feedback."

Suggested items on a meeting agenda:

1. Include a stop and start time.
2. List who will be present.
3. Start with an icebreaker.
4. Review data or relevant metrics for growth.
5. Review goals, both individually and corporately.

6. Share announcements that apply to the team present or that need to ripple out.

7. Review action items from the last meeting.

8. Identify and discuss any issues, ideas, or questions. Create action items if necessary.

9. Conclude by acknowledging who will ripple any information that needs to be shared outside of the meeting.

Icebreakers are a great way to get to know your employees a little better. The Toolbox includes several ideas to spur your conversations.

Use short icebreakers like "This or That?" or "Would You Rather?" in meetings with larger teams that need to move through the group conversation in a timely manner. Let the team know you're going to use a short icebreaker and that you'll move quickly around the room (or online). Ask a simple this-or-that question, such as, "Coffee or tea?" or "Hiking or biking?"

"Would you rather skydive or snow ski?" or "Would you rather read a book or watch a movie?" Keep the additional chatter to a minimum but allow people to connect with each other based on their answers.

In smaller groups, you can use prompts that have a bit longer response such as, "Share a win for the week," or "Share a business best and a personal best for the week." Get to know your team on a deeper level, especially your Leadership Team and/or people you trust with confidential information. Ask questions about emotional experiences or memories, such as, "Share about a time you felt fearful," or "Share how you felt about our last meeting or marketing campaign."

If your group has worked together for some time, you could ask them to write three words that describe the leadership qualities they see in the person to their right (or assign names if using video chat). It can be powerful to know how others see you.

Don't neglect breaking the ice as it eases tension and sets the tone for a meeting. It also shows your team that you recognize that they are real people with real feelings and personalities.

Leadership Meetings

Leadership meetings are for the top leaders in your organization. These can be department heads or your Executive Team. The idea is to have someone from each department represented. If your company is large enough to have an Operations Officer, this person usually oversees multiple departments and will ripple the information out in their department meetings. If your company structure is correct, you'll never have two people from the same department in a leadership meeting.

Here are some of the biggest mistakes we've seen at leadership meetings:

1. Having a department meeting inside of the leadership meeting—If an issue should be resolved at the departmental level, have the appropriate leader take it back to that department's meeting. Don't hijack your leadership meeting time by talking about a marketing plan that should be discussed in your marketing meeting.

2. Not actually solving the root problem or assigning responsibility—Don't check items off your agenda that haven't been assigned or completed.

3. A team member in presentation mode before an idea has been discussed—If your company is collaborative, meetings should be as well.

Annual Planning Meetings

Once a year, your Leadership Team should spend a day or two working *on* the business, not *in* the business. Take time away from day-to-day operations to plan your company goals for the year. Keeping your company goals in alignment with your Vision will help with retention, and you need to take the time to plan *where* you are going and *how* you are going to get there.

This meeting should conclude with the yearly goals separated by quarter—what can be accomplished in the first quarter, the second quarter, and so on. After goals have been established by the team, the information should be assimilated into the departments. Each person responsible for a portion of the goal will use a Goal MAP to clearly define their part and the milestones to complete it. Focus on mapping the first quarter while understanding how the goals fit in the yearly picture. Subsequent quarters will be planned in quarterly meetings discussed next.

Quarterly Planning Meetings

Three times per year, your Leadership Team should meet to plan quarterly goals for the company based on the annual goals, established in the above-mentioned Annual Planning Meeting. The three-month time period works best as it allows time to achieve the goals alongside day-to-day operations, but it isn't so long that your team will lose focus. Again, after goals have been established by the team, the information should be assimilated into the departments. Each person responsible for a portion of the goal will use a Goal MAP to clearly define their part and the milestones to complete it.

Department Meetings

Each department should conduct regular meetings. How often? That depends on the department and the material covered during the meeting. Set an appropriate meeting frequency. Don't assume you need a weekly meeting which could waste your team's valuable time. If your meetings aren't producing tasks, to-dos, or changes, the information can be delivered via an announcement.

If your company is large, you may have sub-departmental meetings as well. For example, if you have a sizable Sales Department with distinct lines of business, each line may hold its own meeting if warranted to discuss product improvements or specific issues with the sales of that product.

When deciding who will attend which meetings, the key is to avoid overlap. If someone works in multiple departments, you may consider a restructure rather than require that person to spend time in multiple meetings discussing the same topic with different people.

Company-wide Meetings

These will vary depending on the size of your company. The objective of a company-wide meeting is twofold:

1. Team communication (successes, goals, Vision-casting, and updates)
2. Team-building (Promotes Core Values and encourages collaboration)

As with any meeting, have a clear agenda, respect the time of the participants, and ripple information as needed to vendors, clients, or team members that weren't present.

Direct Report Meetings

Depending on the size of your company and your current position, you may or may not have direct reports. If you do, you'll schedule quarterly and annual meetings, ensuring they are on track with their goals and gathering feedback and input from their perspective. The majority of feedback should come to you from your direct report meetings utilizing the Quarterly and Annual Direct Report

ScoreCARDs and Capacity Checks (more on both later in this chapter).

Response Meetings

An example of a response meeting would be meeting with individual team members to follow up after sending a company-wide Capacity Check. When setting up the meeting, clearly communicate the intention. If you have an HR Department or Hiring Manager, they should conduct this meeting, as a shift in employee responsibilities may be the next step.

Client Meetings

Client meetings should have a clear agenda as well. Letting your client know what to expect is respectful and will allow them to invite the right people from their team.

Don't call your team into any meetings, especially with a client, already in progress without giving them a heads up on why you are meeting, what you need them for, and what goal you are trying to achieve. We've been blindsided by meetings before, and nothing will discredit a leader faster than this continued behavior. No one likes to be caught off guard. Setting your team up to succeed shows respect for them and the positions they hold. Prepare your team with as much information as possible before going into the meeting, including anything that is confidential or shouldn't be shared with the client. Don't assume they know.

Treat your team like you want your team to treat your clients. As with any situation, your lack of preparation or lack of preparing your team doesn't give you the right to treat them with disrespect. Your unpreparedness is not your team's emergency to fix.

Ripple Communication

Ripple communication is any information that will affect other team members, contractors, specialists, vendors, or clients. Assigning one point person to share specific information across departments, outside the company, and so on, will ensure accuracy of the information. If the ripple comes from the Annual or Quarterly Planning Meeting, it will likely be shared at a company-wide meeting and then on a more granular level in department meetings, if applicable.

Promises made to clients but not communicated to your team ahead of time lack a process or supportive infrastructure which causes confusion and leads to potential mistakes. Before you email or post publicly, your team should not only know what you will communicate publicly but also the appropriate answers to FAQs, applicable links, or other resources needed to support your clients.

Any information from the meetings we mentioned before that needs to be communicated to those outside of the meetings should be rippled out. Sometimes you can simply meet with department heads and have them share the information with their teams; other times, if appropriate, you can share the information across your internal communication platform. The key, as with any communication, is consistency. Set up a weekly update or quick video broadcast with reminders, recapping announcements or alerting the company of what's to come.

Changes to the internal team or structure of the company should be shared appropriately.

Is everyone made aware of policy changes? What about branding or staff changes? Does the team know you're changing the company logo? You'll make them wonder about job security if things change but aren't properly communicated. This is especially the case for anything that financially affects the team, such as changes in payroll or pay periods. Start

Ripple communication consistently.

miscommunicating your team's finances, and they will start looking for a more secure place to work.

This leads us to the all-important topic of hiring and firing. All changes to the team need to be announced—the good and the bad, the growing or the shrinking. We discuss at length in the first two books of this series all the reasons why you should communicate open job positions and new hires with your team. You will also read in *The Exit Process* why communicating someone's exit is just as important. Honest communication can stop rumors or questions before they begin.

Feedback, Reviews, and Discipline

Feedback to and from your team is essential to growth. It's important that you know how to give and receive feedback. Constructive criticism is *still* criticism. The term is overused and usually leaves people feeling criticized, constructively or not. Avoid using it when possible and talk about feedback instead.

Supervisors need to know their teams as individuals to understand what motivates them and what type of feedback works—both positive and negative. Communicate it in the way they are most likely to hear and receive it. Feedback is an opportunity, not a threat. It should come with specific examples instead of vague generalizations.

Your team will also be more likely to hear your feedback if they have witnessed you receiving it or been given the opportunity to give you feedback. Understand that it is hard for employees to give feedback to those above them in the hierarchy of the business. This takes trust, value, and respect. Listen when your team speaks, even if you don't agree. Acknowledge their point of view and discuss solutions openly. Be genuine in your praise and sincere in your correction. (We'll speak more about discipline in a moment.)

Before you offer feedback, be certain the issue isn't due to your lack of leadership. If it is, own it. Discuss the issue and take responsibility. Identify the changes needed to avoid it in the future.

While you want to create a culture that allows for feedback on a regular basis, here are three specific ways to engage in feedback with your employees:

1. Capacity Check
2. Quarterly Direct Report Meeting
3. Annual Direct Report Meeting (Performance Review)

Capacity Check

As small businesses grow, it's not uncommon for leaders to fall out of touch with their team. Focusing on the growth of a business can distract from the internal people component. Sometimes growth happens so quickly that the immediate thought is to continue hiring more team members, without pausing to think about the retention of current team members.

To avoid being out of touch with your team—and to escape unnecessary costly hires—conduct a Capacity Check annually or before beginning the hiring process for a new position. In *The Hiring Process,* we look at the Capacity Check from the perspective of hiring. For this book, we look through the lens of team health and retention. A thorough Capacity Check can increase team health, decrease turnover, and eliminate unnecessary hiring. All these save your business money as well as time and headaches.

Time comes to mind first when discussing the capacity of your team. But capacity is more than available work hours. It is also the capacity of skill sets, experience, and growth. You can assess these components by developing a survey that gathers your team's input.

A word of caution: Don't attempt a Capacity Check until you are ready to act on the responses. Asking for feedback but not acknowledging it will hurt your relationship with team members and harm your company culture.

Here are three reasons to conduct a Capacity Check annually, that support employee retention:

1. Pinpoint what motivates team members.
2. Identify if a team member is overwhelmed with their current workload.
3. Determine gaps in communication or tools needed for your team to perform well.

Develop Questions

Start with the goal in mind when writing the questions for your Capacity Check. You'll want to know about skill sets, time, experience, and growth.

Here are some suggested Capacity Check questions that relate to employee retention:

- What job role, duties, or day-to-day tasks do you find fascinating and motivating?
- Are you satisfied with your current workload? Or do you have the capacity and desire for more?
- Do you have a skill set that isn't being utilized? If so, what are these skills?
- Do you have access to everything you need to perform to the best of your ability?
- Do you feel that your job allows you to develop new skills?

Always include an open-ended question at the end. This can be used as a catch-all for any items the employee wants to share but were not previously addressed. For example, "Do you have any other input, suggestions, or ideas you'd like to share with the Leadership Team?" Remember, allowing opportunities for feedback is vital to keeping a team healthy.

Distribute to the Team

Once you have developed your questions, it is time to distribute them to the team. Begin by sharing your motivation for asking. Reference your Core Values and how the Capacity Check questions relate to supporting and protecting the Core Components of the business. Focus on the need for honest and well-thought-out responses. Give a deadline, and follow up with those who don't submit their Capacity Check. This follow-up conveys the message that each team member's input is valued.

Be upfront about who will be reviewing the responses. Ideally, this should only be your

Leadership Team. For team members to feel that their feedback is confidential, they need to know who will (or won't) be reviewing it.

Analyze Results

It's likely that you already know much of what will be shared, and many of the responses won't require action on your part. When analyzing the results, highlight those items that do require action, such as a team member who

- wants more hours.
- shares that work isn't evenly distributed among their team.
- has a skill set that isn't utilized in their current role but could be in another department.
- points to communication issues that cause them to not fully understand their responsibilities.

These findings will help you identify the strengths and weaknesses of your team. Be thick-skinned when reviewing these responses. Open and honest feedback can be tough to hear. Don't consider any pain points as attacks; instead, see them as opportunities to grow and retain a valuable employee.

Act on It

Thank the entire team for their feedback. Let them know that you value it and plan to act on it where necessary. This will strengthen relationships with your team. Follow up with individuals who have concerns worthy of exploration. Never ignore a major claim or concern. If the team member felt it was worth sharing, then it is worth acknowledging.

For those who express interest in or capacity for additional or different work, develop a plan to further assess these skills before moving them into the new roles according to your OAR Chart. As a Leadership Team, identify any overarching issues and plan to address them immediately. This is where holding yourself accountable to Core Values or company culture is a necessity.

Lastly, keep the responses handy for reference. Review them during annual reviews and when dealing with disciplinary issues or as other problems arise.

Team Capacity Check

1. What job role, duties, or day-to-day tasks do you find irritating?
2. What job role, duties, or day-to-day tasks do you find to just be OK?
3. What job role, duties, or day-to-day tasks do you find fascinating and motivating?
4. Do you find your workload reasonable?
5. Are you satisfied with your current workload? Or have the capacity and desire for more hours or projects?
6. Do you believe work is distributed evenly across your team?
7. How would you rate the way our organization makes use of your strengths?
8. Do you have a skill set that isn't being utilized? If so, what?
9. Is there an area of the company that you are interested in learning more about?
10. Are your responsibilities clear to you and those you work with?
11. Do you have access to everything you need to perform to the best of your ability?
12. Do you have the appropriate amount of information to make correct decisions about your work including feedback?
13. How would you rate communication in our organization?
14. Do you feel that you are growing professionally?
15. Do you feel that your job allows you to develop new skills?
16. Do you see a path to advance your career in our company?
17. Which Core Value do you relate to most and why?
18. What do you want to be remembered for?
19. In what ways do you like to be recognized? Financially, public praise, gifts, rewards, special activities?
20. Do you have any other input, suggestions, or ideas you'd like to share with the Leadership Team?

Quarterly and Annual Direct Report ScoreCARDs

Leaders should meet with each of their direct reports one-on-one four times a year. This is one reason why we previously advised to limit a leader's number of direct reports.

We will describe the different types of meetings you'll have, at which you'll use these tools:

- Agenda
- Quarterly or Annual Direct Report ScoreCard (QDR and ADR respectively)
- Goal MAP

If you've read the first two books in this series, the ScoreCARD will look familiar to you. You've seen the Interview ScoreCard and the Onboarding ScoreCard, and now you will use a modified version four times per year—three times during Quarterly Direct Report (QDR)

Meetings and one at the Annual Direct Report (ADR) Meeting. Pay close attention to how you use it differently in each of the following meetings. Both Direct Report ScoreCARDs can be found in the Toolbox. See the completed examples here.

Quarterly Direct Report ScoreCARD

Employee Name <u>Brad Robbins</u> **Date** <u>10/6/22</u>

Rate on a 1-10 scale (in the box provided).
Provide a specific example (positive or negative) for each.

☐10☐ **C**ulture –I feel the workplace culture is healthy and positive.
<u>Absolutely! It is evident how much the Leadership Team puts into</u>
<u>making sure employees feel valued and appreciated for their work.</u>

☐9☐ **A**bility–I have the feedback, time, and tools to do my job to the best of my ability.
<u>Regular check-ins with my supervisor have provided constructive</u>
<u>feedback for how I can adjust and improve to do my best.</u>

☐9☐ **R**ole–I see how my role supports the company's bigger Vision and Mission.
<u>Using the Goal MAP and seeing how my individual goals support the</u>
<u>current company goals is beneficial for seeing the big picture.</u>

☐7☐ **D**esire–I'm satisfied with my current role and responsibilities.
<u>I enjoy my role and team greatly. But I would love more</u>
<u>opportunities to grow within the company.</u>

Has your role changed over the last quarter?	Yes	(No)
Do you feel like the culture aligns with the Company's Core Components?	(Yes)	No
Are the Core Values evident in the day-to-day operations of the company?	(Yes)	No
Do you feel that information is clearly communicated throughout the company?	(Yes)	No
Are you given opportunities to give input and share feedback?	(Yes)	No

Other notes or explanation of answers above:
<u>Specifically on the topic of communication - I've never worked</u>
<u>anywhere that has been so intentional and consistent with how</u>
<u>team communication is handled.</u>

Share an experience or project that excited you this past quarter.
<u>Supporting Carol with the launch last quarter. Its success along with</u>
<u>her praise of my contributions made me feel very accomplished.</u>

Annual Direct Report ScoreCARD

Employee Name _Brad Robbins_   **Hire Date** _3/28/22_

Supervisor conducting review
Carol Burns   **Review Date** _4/3/23_

Does the employee communicate clearly and understand when communicated with? (Yes)   No

Review Goal MAP. Have goals been met? (Yes)   No

If no to either - identify the source of the problem and what corrective steps need to be taken._____N/A_____

Rate on a 1-10 scale (in the box provided).
Provide a specific example (positive or negative) for each.

[10] **C**ulture –does the employee exhibit the Core Values?

Yes. Brad is clearly a lifelong learner and values caloborative thinking. It is evident with all of his team projects.

[8] **A**bility–employee is emotionally, physically, educationally, and intelligently capable of carrying out the responsibilities of their job.

Yes, he has shown competency with all tools needed for his role. He especially exhibits emotional intelligence in how he interacts with both his team and clients.

[9] **R**ole–has the employee shown an understanding of their role, responsibilities, and where they fit into the overall company picture?

Brad is dependable with all of his responsibilities. We discuss specifically how his work supports the team and the company. He is encouraged by seeing the big picture.

[10] **D**esire–does the employee show a desire to continue in this role and to continue working for the company?

Absolutely! Brad has taken the initiative to plan improvements for the next company-wide meeting. Showing his commitment and enthusiasm in how he supports the overall mission.

Additional training needs
_N/A_

Strategies for improvement or growth
Brad continues to be a star team member. We will explore more opportunities in the coming year on how he can grow with his duties as they relate to managing our CRM system.

Quarterly Direct Report Meeting

Some companies call these quarterly reviews, and some have creative names for them. But the important thing about this meeting is that it allows your direct reports to share their perspectives one-on-one with you. We provide an example agenda in the Toolbox to guide you in getting the most out of these meetings. This should be a time for you to openly discuss processes and systems and hear their wins and concerns.

During the meeting, walk your employee through the QDR ScoreCARD. Listen to how they rate each component. They will tell you what is working well in addition to any areas they feel they need support in.

Next, have them review their Goal MAP with you. You may start to see a pattern if they are struggling with their milestones and they've expressed an area in need of support. It's possible that they haven't made the connection yet. Work through milestones, adjusting where needed to help them see a clear path to goal success.

QDR Meetings are important for retention because they keep the leader and the employee on the same page in regard to the role and expectations.

Annual Direct Report Meeting

Consider Annual Direct Report Meetings your annual performance reviews. Information received during QDR meetings will prepare you well to give your review. Never ask an employee to write their own review. This is the time to recap the year with them. What goals have they accomplished? What Core Values have you seen them demonstrate consistently?

Use the example ADR Meeting Agenda provided in the Toolbox to structure your meeting and cover all relevant information. Prior to meeting with your employee, you'll complete the ADR ScoreCARD from your perspective, then discuss it with them during the meeting. You'll also evaluate the employee's Goal MAP worksheets for the year. This will allow you to see if they are meeting expectations, can take on more aggressive goals in the upcoming year, or need additional support or training. Adjust Goal MAP milestones and metrics as applicable.

Make sure the annual review is not the only basis for pay raises. While you will take this information into consideration, raises should be given based on company profitability as well as employee performance. If the company is losing money, you'll need to correct this issue and compensate your employees in a way that makes sense. If the employee's performance warrants a raise, now would be the time to communicate what the raise is and when it will go into effect.

Always collaborate with your HR and Finance Manager prior to extending the offer.

Discipline

As adults, we view discipline as either something negative or a necessary part of growth. Regardless of your perspective, discipline must be practiced to keep your culture healthy. If you read *The Onboarding Process*, you established your disciplinary policy when setting other policies. If your company does not have a disciplinary policy, now is the time to create one. Discuss with your Leadership Team and create policies that ensure discipline is equal across your company.

Most importantly, handle disciplinary issues immediately. Don't wait until the QDR or ADR Meetings to discipline. You can discuss or reiterate the issues at those meetings, but action should be taken at the time of the incident. Delaying consequences would be equivalent to disciplining your child once a quarter for bad behavior that occurred almost ninety days ago. Take immediate action appropriate to the issue at hand.

While you don't have to fix or solve the issue yourself, talk through it to gain clarity. You may ask your employee what they could possibly do differently in the future and brainstorm some ideas together. But don't expect them to correct poor behavior just because you point it out. They may not know how to make the changes, which is why they haven't. Remember, it is your responsibility to lead them. Don't make being likable a priority over difficult conversations, which are sometimes inevitable.

The techniques you use depend on the situation. Sometimes it is easier to have a difficult conversation over the phone, avoiding emotional body language or possible tears. At other times, it's better to be in person, eye to eye, so you can see reactions and emotions. We don't suggest being vulnerable in email or interoffice communication; verbal communication is always best.

Consider the following when it comes to discipline in the workplace:

1. Make sure that consequences are applicable to the situation.
2. Be prepared for potential fallout if discipline isn't well received.
3. Understand that words are like toothpaste—once they are out, you can't put them back in.

Allow appropriate vulnerability when disciplining. We believe vulnerability builds trust. Trust leads to retention. The best solution for disciplinary issues is discovering the root of the problem, and you may have to be vulnerable when digging up that issue. As we discussed in Chapter 2, if you can be flexible, make adjustments to avoid issues in the future.

Using proper operational communication, as you can see, impacts company culture. Put forth the effort to establish and implement a solid infrastructure. You, your team, and your clients will all benefit from it.

Chapter Six

Invest in Your Team

You don't inspire your teammates by showing them how amazing you are. You inspire them by showing them how amazing they are.

—Roby Benincasa

Compensation

Money matters. Let's not pretend for a moment that your team would work for free. Even in the most ideal company culture, people still have to pay their bills and provide for their families. Financial compensation should be competitive. Pay people what they are worth. Your HR Department should be in the know about the going rate for certain positions and set pay rates accordingly.

Think Outside the Paycheck

As we discussed in Chapter 1, a company's culture is shaped by its values and daily actions. Culture is more about relationships than perks, though the perks do play a supporting role. The tone is set by the leaders of the business. You can positively change your company culture and discover how to best invest in your team by being in tune with them. Listen, communicate, and build relationships. Learn what they care about, what motivates them, and what frustrates them. Then take action to create a culture of worth based on what you learn.

When businesses invest in their people, a positive culture will emerge, and you will see returns on that investment. Increased productivity and satisfied customers will improve revenue. Employee retention will greatly decrease the costly expense of turnover. All of these consequences positively impact your company's profitability.

There is no one-size-fits-all solution for investing in your team. Communication and understanding what is important to them are critical when deciding how to invest in your team.

Here are four ways you could invest in your team:

1. Career development plan—Show your team that you are committed to their continued growth and learning.

2. Wellness programs (both physical and mental)—Healthy people will perform better at work.

3. Recognition program to reward achievers—But provide rewards they really want and will appreciate. A company coffee mug is not a reward.

4. Feedback opportunities—The opportunity to voice opinions, questions, and concerns is essential to healthy work relationships.

A great company culture doesn't simply happen by saying you will invest in your team. It takes effort, time, and follow-through. Empty promises of a change in culture will be a detriment to your business.

Training and Tools

Team training and professional development should be looked at as investments, not expenses. Returns on these investments aren't as easy to quantify as traditional investments, but nonetheless, the gains they provide are substantial and irreplaceable. Investing in your team is the best validation.

If you invest resources in a team training or development session, know ahead of time how you will implement it into daily work. The training needs to be meaningful, productive, and valuable. If the training doesn't matter a week later, it was a disruption. If that team training also took the employees away from their families and personal lives, you're disrespecting them on a deeper level. Value their time.

A weekend training for a team that normally doesn't work on the weekends should either come with additional compensation or time off the week before or after. Working anyone straight through their scheduled time off is disrespectful, toxic to your culture, and in some cases against labor laws.

As a business owner, you should invest in the right software, technology, and tools that allow your team to get the job done, but don't forget to invest in your people too. Invest with the right intention and in a way that will produce results. Your people are your most valuable and expensive asset and the most important component to helping you achieve your dreams of a successful business.

Recognition

Share the wins often and publicly. Telling your employee she did a great job behind closed doors is fine, but celebrating her in front of your team and/or clients will go further. This validates her and shows your appreciation for what she brings to the table. This creates a culture of worth. People want to know they matter. As a leader, it is your responsibility to acknowledge how much they do for the company.

Share the wins:

- Acknowledge them publicly.
- Celebrate what you want to replicate.
- Use words of affirmation to encourage your team.
- Find ways for the team to recognize each other.

Use the Company Core Components, especially the Core Values, as a way to recognize your employees. Brenda set up a "Core Value Train" at a remote company. The train starts at the Leadership Team, which recognizes an employee and points out the Core Value they demonstrate. Then the recognized employee follows suit within a week, highlighting someone else and the Core Value they demonstrate. This is done in the interoffice communication all-teams channel. Other team members can comment and continue to build the employee up, creating a succession of acknowledgment. It not only highlights and validates one employee, but it reminds the others of the company's culture and values.

Have your team think creatively about how to recognize employees and how they can in turn recognize each other. It doesn't have to be costly or time-consuming.

While a recognition gift is a nice way to show appreciation, the gift should fit the achievement you're recognizing the employee for. Don't forget to use the Fun Fact Form (found in the Toolbox) as well to make sure you're rewarding with gifts that make them feel known.

Some employees on social media had this to say about their company recognition gifts. One post read, "My company sent me a cup and a pack of mints to thank me for my five years ... I'm headed to Indeed as we speak." (If you're not aware, Indeed is an online job board.)

Here are some of the comments that followed:

*You will be snatched up in this market hopefully by
an employer that appreciates your service more than a logo cup.*

*A five-year paperweight and a mousepad. I work in digital
entertainment so … little-to-no paper and we all use trackpads …*

I got a shout-out in the monthly newsletter for 10 years.

My husband got a chip clip for teaching in his district for 5 years.

*I got 600 points for 10 YEARS, which is basically Monopoly money
you can spend on a prize-selection website. On my 11th anniversary,
I got no points, because "you only get them every five years."*

*I got a mirror to put on my desk so I can
"make sure others can hear my smile" in meetings …*

I got an American flag pin for five years …

*I got a $5 Starbucks gift card for seven years
and also brought in more new sales than our VP of sales
for the year. Spoiler alert, I'm not in sales.*

*I got a Hershey bar as a bonus
at a billion-dollar corporation 9 years ago lol.*

I got a letter in the mail and that's it.

*I got an ink pen with a compass on the cap. *blank stare*
I used that compass to find a new job. 11 years.*

*Certificate of appreciation for five years of service
at a multi-billion-dollar logistics company.*

You got something?

*But did you get a pin AND a shout-out in a thread with everyone
else who had an anniversary the same month? 22 YEARS.*

*Not to brag, but it depends on the time of year. We get mugs
or some type of insulated cup, a very see-through and
inappropriate t-shirt, and some other things that don't really
make sense. But what we don't get are well-earned raises for all
of the bs that we do that is outside of our job description.*

*We used to get cups on our anniversary. Now we get a
"commemorative coin." At least the cup was functional.*

Do you hear how devalued these employees feel? For years, they have worked—some going above and beyond—but received no recognition or the wrong recognition. It doesn't matter the size of the organization, as we've seen it in all businesses.

So, what do you do? Recognition and appreciation can be expressed in many ways. It comes down to respect. Respect their time, skills, boundaries, personal life, and future, and you'll have loyal employees.

Respecting people's time is one of the most important ways you can show value.

Brenda once worked for a company that decided it would be a great idea for her and her two male colleagues to start their colleagues to start their

It comes down to respect.

day at the gym together and then conduct their morning meeting in the lobby after they showered and dressed. The company thought they were creating a positive culture. What they created was a hassle and an inappropriate inconvenience. Brenda had to cut her workouts short to allow time to get ready and be at the meeting on time. She also had to cart more personal items to the gym to dress professionally every day.

It wasn't convenient. It didn't build the culture they'd hoped for. The company portrayed the free gym membership as a gift. But gifts don't come with rules. Think through the gifts you are giving and ask yourself, "Does this respect the employee's time, skills, boundaries, and/or personal life?"

If your company plans retreats away from the daily norm, do you pay the staff during the retreats? Are the retreats included and explained in their Job Description? Define retreat. Is it really team training disguised as fun so you don't have to pay them? If you asked your employees what would make them feel special, each one would have an answer through the lens of their experiences and current circumstances. You should consider both before pulling someone away from their family or personal life to a getaway you consider fun in the name of team-building.

Guidelines for employee appreciation and recognition:

- Respect processes. Stay in your lane.
- A small raise is better than no raise.
- Use the Capacity Check (Chapter 5) and discuss feedback.
- Honor boundaries. Especially work hours, for remote employees.
- Set up a reward system that allows the employee to choose their gift.
- Create a system to check on employees when out for illness, extended leave, or other reasons.
- Properly train your employees. Letting them look like fools in front of a client only makes you look like a fool.

- Give gifts that show you actually care—that you see their potential—gifts unique to the individual. Not everyone gets a popcorn bucket.
- Set up a company calendar and include birthdays. It's a simple way to show recognition and care. Send/give a gift or hand-written card.

A leader cares for the whole employee, not just who they are during working hours. Allow people to be authentic at work. Create an environment of acceptance.

Happy Employees, Happy Clients

Staff turnover may cause concern with your clients, and how you treat your clients may cause staff turnover. The two go hand in hand. Your team sees how you treat your clients. Be sure your behavior is aligned with your values.

We mentioned cutting corners earlier, but it is worth mentioning again in this context. If your team sees you cutting corners that could harm the client or produce an insufficient product, they will quickly lose respect for you and how you conduct business. Treat your clients and your employees the way you would want to be treated. Your clients see your culture too. Don't compromise. Honor your employees in front of your clients and never blame them if something goes wrong. If your team makes a mistake, own it from a leadership standpoint. Correct it privately and protect your culture.

Celebrate your clients and your team publicly, if appropriate. View both relationships as lifetime partnerships, not a one-time transaction or someone just getting a job done. Your goal is long-term employees who love your company and will tell the world. This will assist in long-term relationships with your clients and, more importantly, lead to repeat business. Happy clients will tell the world about you as well. Happy employees and clients will save you valuable marketing dollars and maintain your culture of worth. If you can set up a client referral or loyalty program, do so. Your employees will see the organic growth of the business and feel good about working for your company.

One unhappy client or employee on social media or in circles of influence can do irreparable damage to your business. Protect your culture from all angles. Remember, you started your business to solve people's problems. Set proper expectations and live up to them, and you'll win on both fronts—happy clients and retained employees.

Mentor

Creating a mentorship program promotes collaboration, strengthens your company culture, and provides an opportunity to keep your high performers engaged and committed to the company. On the mentee side, it provides support and connection. As we covered in *The Onboarding Process,* mentorship can be a significantly useful tool for new hires. But when viewing it from a retention perspective, we also see the benefits for the mentor. A mentee is not the only one who learns and grows during these relationships.

Being selected as a mentor conveys to your employee that you see them performing well, that you trust them, and that they are an important part of the team. This opportunity gives the mentor a sense of ownership and pride. Mentors become better communicators and leaders. All of this leads to improved job satisfaction and retention.

>>>>>>

Imagine a team that shows up promptly to work each day. They are feeling happy to be there, are pleasant to work with, own their responsibilities, and leave satisfied at the end of the day. They become loyal to your company and appreciative of the training and growth opportunities provided to them. Their work-life balance is protected. The thought of searching for a different job never crosses their mind. This team is working in an excellent culture of worth, and they will keep doing so as long as they feel valued. All of this is possible when you invest in your team.

Chapter Seven

Wrap-up and Resources

*If everyone is moving forward together,
then success takes care of itself.*

—Henry Ford

As you've read in the previous six chapters, retention takes effort. If the whole team hasn't been rowing together toward the same destination, it will take time to change the direction of your organization. The good news is that any effort applied toward retention strengthens your business in other ways as well. With intention and deliberate focus, you can align your team with your

Vision and collaborate with them to make great progress toward reaching it.

While verbal and written communication is important, the biggest factor in retention is how you communicate with actions.

We've provided you with tools to clarify written and verbal communication and to

What are your actions communicating?

create a culture of worth through actions. If you read this book with your team, you may have started to already implement these processes. If you haven't, now is the time to get the team on board.

At your next Leadership Team meeting, introduce the book and the concept of a culture of worth in your workplace. Have your Leadership Team read this book and set a time to discuss the areas where your company needs to improve. You may want to schedule time during your existing

Leadership Team meetings to discuss which tools you'll implement and when, or it may serve your team better to designate another meeting to thoroughly dive into the content. Either way, remember that it takes action. Map out a plan with your team.

We introduced you to new tools, like the Workplace Culture Assessment and Company Core Components Worksheet, while diving deeper into more familiar tools, like the Goal MAP, Capacity Check, and ScoreCARDs. Determine which team members will own these—implementing, training, and answering questions. They will be the go-to for each tool. Some tools will naturally fall to HR or another specific department. Others will be used company-wide, like the Goal MAP. Assigning one person to take ownership of training will ensure that your team fully understands and is utilizing the tool correctly—rowing together. If applicable, add this responsibility to the assigned box on the OAR Chart. This will communicate to your team who to direct questions to when a new tool is rolled out.

You'll also want to implement any company-wide changes that arise as a result of a new tool. For example, if you've made changes to your Company Core Components, ripple the information to the Tech Team to update the website, the Marketing Team to utilize in advertising, HR to update the Team Handbook, and so on.

When implementing QDR meetings, make sure all your supervisors and leads understand that this meeting is for the employee to be heard, not the other way around. Designating one person to train all your leaders on conducting this meeting and using the QDR ScoreCARD will provide clarity and unity.

Discuss with your leaders the best ways to invest in your team. Is there a particular need for company-wide training or training in a certain department? Brainstorm new recognition standards. Will you recognize based on the Core Values? Who will roll this out and keep it on track?

We get it. There are many moving parts in a culture of worth. Once you establish the flow of new processes and systems, it will continue in the smooth rhythm of the infinity symbol. Depending on the size of your company, you may make a goal to implement one new tool per quarter, or even per year. Don't feel pressure to do this all yourself or all at once. If you need outside training or a workshop to walk your team through these tools, don't hesitate to reach out to us at thejoyofpursuit.com/workwithus.

That's a Wrap!

As a final wrap-up, let's do a quick recap that will add clarity and act as your retention checklist.

Our Company Core Components are

- ☐ clear and aligned with each other.
- ☐ in alignment with our daily actions.
- ☐ communicated in multiple ways to the team on a regular basis.
- ☐ included in our Brand Guide and used in marketing.
- ☐ used as a filter for all actions, product creations, and major decisions.

Leaders in our organization understand the importance of

- ☐ setting and respecting boundaries.
- ☐ process ownership.
- ☐ avoiding micromanagement.
- ☐ stress management.
- ☐ emotional intelligence and how it applies to the role.

Our company is legally and legitimately structured with

- ☐ clear SOPs in place.
- ☐ on-going quality control.
- ☐ generous benefits.
- ☐ safety and compliance.
- ☐ training and cross-training.
- ☐ privacy protection.
- ☐ a solid financial plan and implemented budget.

We have proper accountability in every level of our company through

- ☐ our OAR Chart.
- ☐ ownership of responsibilities and mistakes.
- ☐ tracking proper metrics that reflect company-wide health.
- ☐ strategically mapped goals that align with our bigger Vision.
- ☐ anticipation of needs across the company and goals.

There are clear communication channels in place to

- ☐ conduct productive meetings.
- ☐ adequately plan annual goals.
- ☐ check the capacity of our team on a regular basis.
- ☐ track quarterly goals and collect feedback from our team.
- ☐ discipline in a timely and professional manner according to the policies in place.

We understand that investing in our team means more than a paycheck, and we add value to our team with a commitment to

- ☐ fair compensation.
- ☐ a standard benefits package.
- ☐ benefits beyond the standard.
- ☐ client referral program.
- ☐ a mentor program.
- ☐ recognition programs that highlight our Core Values.

We value
- ☐ simplified operations to maximize efficiency and communication.
- ☐ invested, committed employees in a culture of worth.
- ☐ retention of valued employees, resources, and revenue.

Throughout this process for retention, we've shared strategies, standards, and tools to help you create the culture of worth your team needs and deserves. As with any knowledge, it must be applied to be transformative. Remember your actions are speaking. Be intentional about what your actions say about you, your company, and how you value those around you.

Download The Retention Process Toolbox at

TheJoyofPursuit.com/Retention

- VPS Guide
- Company Core Components Worksheet
- Icebreakers
- Capacity Check
- Quarterly Direct Report ScoreCARD
- Quarterly Direct Report Meeting Agenda
- Annual Direct Report ScoreCARD
- Annual Direct Report Meeting Agenda
- Goal MAP
- Fun Fact Form
- Workplace Culture Assessment

Acknowledgments

We stand in awe of what God continues to do through this series. Our worth comes from Him and Him alone. We pray this book creates a culture of worth in workplaces around the world that honor the unique souls He created.

We sincerely thank the bosses and leaders that never put us in vulnerable positions, always encouraged us, believed in us, and shaped us into the women in business we are today.

To our family, friends, colleagues, and readers, thank you for your ongoing support. Here's to joy in your pursuits!

A special thanks to Jenifer. I love you more than you'll ever know. Thank you for always being my biggest supporter.—Brenda

Amanda is known both personally and professionally for her consistency, clarity, and commitment. Her grace-given gifts of practicality and focus allow her to keep an accurate perspective in life and business. She is level-headed and gives attention to the necessary priorities without distractions slowing her down. Amanda is an action-taker with a well-thought-out plan of attack in hand.

Throughout her work history, Amanda has frequently been known as the most dependable team member. She began her career with numbers and finances but grew to discover a passion for the people-side of business in Human Resources. She has a talent for identifying uniqueness in others, encouraging them to know their worth and abilities, all while gracefully holding them accountable for their actions.

Despite years of working for a publishing company, Amanda never thought she would be an author. She is now a four-time published author with an entire series for small businesses. *The Team Solution Series: HR Coaching to Grow Teams and Profit* provides more than ideas—the books are full implementation plans to guide you and your team through the employee journey. The content blends Amanda's unparalleled organizational skills with her knowledge of HR practices. Her exceptional ability to improve efficiency and processes in organizations will serve countless small business owners and strengthen their teams.

Throughout the writing and publishing process of *The Team Solution Series* (and thanks to being business partners with a top-notch book coach), Amanda knows that if she can write a book, anyone can. Together with her business partner, Brenda Haire, they created the Author Business Network, providing authors with the tools needed to successfully write, publish, market, and build a business around their books.

Amanda and her two children live at the foothills of the Smoky Mountains in Tennessee. She enjoys hiking with her kids, cooking, and gardening, especially cultivating flowers. She's known for having some of the most beautiful blooms in town. One of the greatest joys of her life is watching her children grow and guiding them to pursue their passions.

Connect with Amanda
LinkedIn.com/in/AmandaJPainter

Brenda's had over forty jobs and has been working since she was twelve. She's never been fired and is not ashamed of her work history. Brenda always worked her way up, out, and on to the next adventure. Many see this as risky and call her fearless. She would tell you that fear was always a factor—she just chose faith instead.

After being told she was a nobody by a publisher, Brenda struggled with her identity as a writer. Not one to give up, she pursued her dream and released her first book, *Save the Butter Tubs!: Discover Your Worth in a Disposable World*, in 2018.

Brenda was immediately hired by her publishing agency after her book was released, and she went on to become the president of the company. An entrepreneur at heart, once again she left on top and now uses her experience to serve individuals and small businesses around the world as the CEO and cofounder of Joy of Pursuit. Brenda created the Author Business Network with her business partner,

Amanda Painter, and together they help authors build businesses around their books.

As a speaker, Brenda shares keynotes and workshops that transform audiences. Whether she is speaking about purpose, publishing, or small business, her deepest desire is to help you shine your light by operating in your grace-given gifts. She considers herself a moved soul—so moved by her encounters with God that she can't help but move in response. She wants the same for you—to encounter God in a way that you can't help but live a life worthy of your calling.

She and her hubs (as she lovingly refers to him on social media), Darren, are both military veterans. They enjoy hiking and chasing waterfalls across the United States and live in Texas with their beautifully blended and expanding family.

Connect with Brenda
Facebook.com/BrendaHaire
Instagram.com/BrendaAHaire
LinkedIn.com/in/Brenda Haire

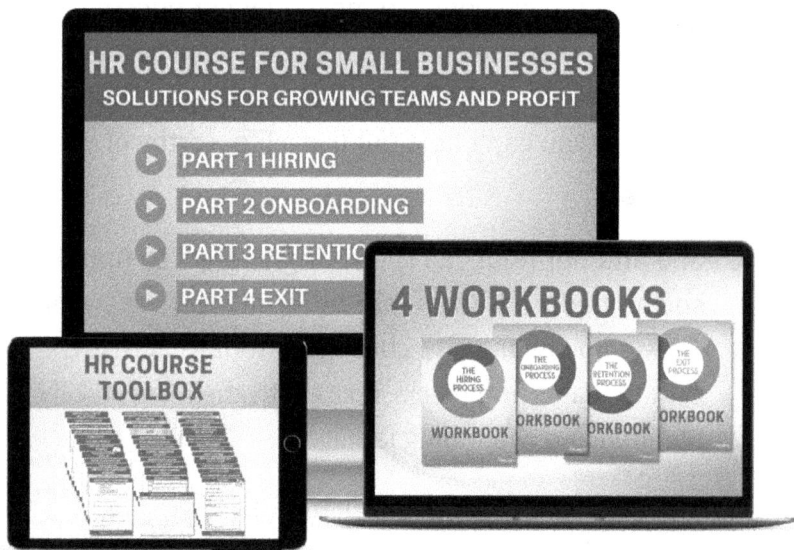

Empower Your Team
Elevate Your Business

» Strategies to Find and Keep Top Talent.

» Techniques that Boost Employee Engagement and Reduce Turnover.

» Tools to Ensure Smooth Transitions and Protect Your Business.

HR COURSE FOR SMALL BUSINESSES
SOLUTIONS FOR GROWING TEAMS AND PROFIT

- PART 1 HIRING
- PART 2 ONBOARDING
- PART 3 RETENTION
- PART 4 EXIT

HR COURSE TOOLBOX

4 WORKBOOKS

THE HIRING PROCESS WORKBOOK

THE ONBOARDING PROCESS WORKBOOK

THE RETENTION PROCESS WORKBOOK

THE EXIT PROCESS WORKBOOK

Unlock the Full Potential
of Your Team » ENROLL NOW

TheJoyofPursuit.com/HR-Course

Revolutionize Your Business
with Our HR Consulting Services

Executive Consultant

Amanda J. Painter

Tailored Solutions for Your HR Challenges

》 Streamline Processes

》 Boost Productivity

》 Reduce Costs

Start Today!

TheJoyOfPursuit.com/
store/p/HRconsult

Receive Exclusive HR Insights, Industry News, and Best Practices Straight to Your Inbox.

CUT THE CHAOS

One email per month to take you and your business from tired and busy to thriving and productive!

Try it today

Tools.TheJoyOfPursuit.com/CutTheChaos

Take the next step in creating a culture of growth and fulfillment of purpose.

COMPLETE THE
TEAM SOLUTION SERIES

TheJoyOfPursuit.com/Books

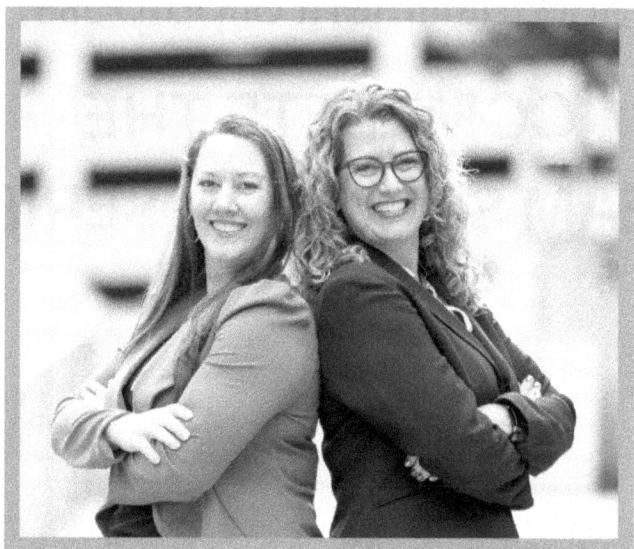

Transform Your Workplace

Build a Custom Workshop for Your Team

Higher Productivity
Efficient Meetings
Lower Turnover
Engaged Employees
Cohesive Leadership Team

It's Time to Create a
Joyful Workplace
for YOU and Your Team!

TheJoyOfPursuit.com/Workshops

Buy in Bulk

for Your Human Resource Team, Directors, or Leadership Team

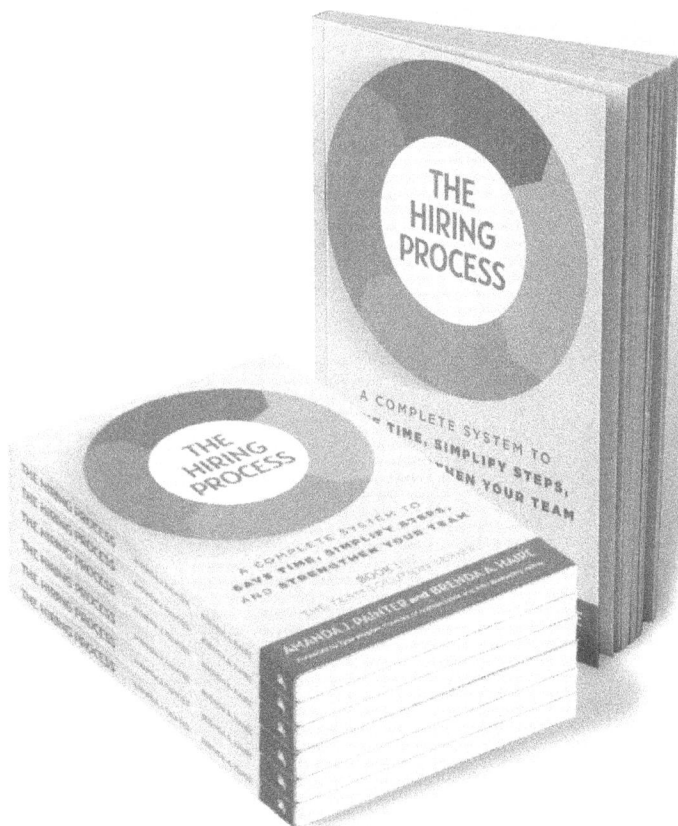

TheJoyofPursuit.com/Books

www.ingramcontent.com/pod-product-compliance
Lightning Source LLC
Chambersburg PA
CBHW071603210326
41597CB00019B/3381